Anonymous

Christianity and Modern Thought

Anonymous

Christianity and Modern Thought

ISBN/EAN: 9783744652384

Printed in Europe, USA, Canada, Australia, Japan

Cover: Foto ©ninafisch / pixelio.de

More available books at **www.hansebooks.com**

THE PRESENT TENSES

OF

THE BLESSED LIFE.

BY

F. B. MEYER, B. A.,

Author of "Abraham: or The Obedience of Faith;"
"Elijah: and the Secret of His Power;" "Israel:
a Prince with God;" etc., etc.

FLEMING H. REVELL COMPANY,
NEW YORK.   CHICAGO.   TORONTO.
Publishers of Evangelical Literature.

PREFACE.

IN a true and deep sense, all who believe have already entered upon the Eternal State. They have stepped across the frontier line into that glorious state of being, in which the changes of this mortal existence cannot affect the permanence of their life or blessedness. "He that believeth on the Son *hath* eternal life."

And it is important for us to remember, that our position does not depend on our experience of it, or on our emotions. These, alas, fluctuate perpetually, now waxing to the full, and again waning to a crescent streak. But we are independent of them on two conditions, which are fundamental to all rest and peace.

In the first place, we must learn to live in our will; and in the second place, we must accustom ourselves to realize—not what we are to God, but—what God is to us, unchangeably, constantly, and in the fulness of a present blessing, which was never less than now in the past, and can never be less in the future. "HE ABIDETH FAITHFUL." Thus we shall find a quiet habitation in the Present Tenses of God's dealing with us—THE PRESENT TENSES OF THE BLESSED LIFE.

F. B. MEYER.

CONTENTS.

I. "I Am With You" 9
II. "My Peace I Give." 18
III. "Cleanseth." 28
IV. "Worketh." 36
V. "Strengtheneth." 44
VI. "Liveth." 53
VII. "Loveth." 62
VIII. "Reigneth." 70
IX. "Teacheth." 77
X. "Comforteth." 86
XI. "The Four-fold Cluster." .. 94
XII. "Our God is a Consuming Fire" 104

CONTENTS.--*Continued.*

XIII. The Spirit's Help." 115

XIV. "The Spirit Lusteth against the Flesh." 123

XV. "Upbraideth Not." 130

XVI. "All Things are Yours." 137

XVII. "Working Together for Good." 146

XVIII. "I am the First and the Last." 157

THE PRESENT TENSES OF THE BLESSED LIFE.

I.

"I Am With You."

MATT. xxviii. 20.

TWO hundred years ago, there lived in the Carmelite Monastery in Paris, a simple-minded man, *who, though a cook by profession, was one of God's rarest jewels. At the age of eighteen, when wandering through a wood, in the depth of winter, the thought was suddenly flashed into his mind, that those very trees, which stood before him naked and bare, would ere long be clothed in all the glory of luxuriant leafage, quivering in the summer breeze. In a moment, he realized that God must be there; and if there, also

* Brother Lawrence.

everywhere; and he said to himself, "He is here, close beside me; and He is everywhere; so that I can never again be out of His holy presence." This sense of the nearness and presence of God became thenceforth one of the formative thoughts of his soul; it never left him for long; and he carefully cultivated it, so that it moulded and fashioned his whole inner being.

It was a noble thought, and it would be of immense assistance to each reader of these lines to acquire an habitual experience of the same kind. But before we can do so, we need a strong foundation on which we can build it up; and surely it would be impossible to find one more suited to our purpose than that contained in those precious words with which our Lord parted from His disciples: "Lo, I AM WITH YOU ALL THE DAYS, EVEN UNTO THE CONSUMMATION OF THE AGE."

How full of meaning is that present

tense! It is not that He *was* with us, or *will be* with us; but that He *is* with us. We may not always see Him, or realize His presence; we may be blinded by our tears, or dazzled with the false glare of this evil world; we may even, like the Lord Himself, in moments of crushing sorrow, reckon ourselves forsaken, and cry out for fear, like startled babes in the dark, who do not know that their mother is sitting by their side; or, like silly children, we may look for our Friend through a reversed telescope, removing Him to an infinite distance by our way of regarding Him. But all this will not alter the fact that He is with us, pitying us, yearning over us, and awaiting the moment when, by a gesture—as to the two at Emmaus—or by the tone of His voice—as to Mary, weeping by the empty grave—He may make us start with the glad consciousness that He is near. Happy the soul which has learnt to say by faith, when it cannot say by feeling, "Thou art near, O Lord." (Psalm cxix. 151.)

"ALL THE DAYS"—in winter days, when joys are fled; in sunless days, when the clouds return again and again after rain; in days of sickness and pain; in days of temptation and perplexity—as much as in days when the heart is as full of joy as the woodlands in spring are full of song. That day never comes when the Lord Jesus is not at the side of His saints. Lover and friend may stand afar; but He walks beside them through the fires; He fords with them the rivers; He stands by them when face to face with the lion. We can never be alone. We must always add His resources to our own, when making our calculations. We may always imagine we hear Him saying, as Alexander did, when his soldiers complained of the overwhelming numbers of the enemy, "How many do you count Me for?"

Now, can we not somehow acquire the habit of recollecting this glorious fact, and of living in its mighty current? I think we may, if we follow these simple directions.

(1) We should never leave our prayer-closets in the morning, without having concentrated our thoughts deeply and intensely on the fact of the actual presence of God: there with us, encompassing us, and filling the room as literally as it fills heaven itself. It may not lead to any distinct results at first; but as we make repeated efforts to realize the presence of God, it will become increasingly real to us. And, as the habit grows upon us—when alone in a room; or when treading the sward of some natural woodland temple; or when pacing the stony street; in the silence of night, or amid the teeming crowds of daylight—we shall

often find ourselves whispering the words: "Thou art near; Thou art here, O Lord."

(2) Then again, we should try to recall the fact of the presence of God whenever we enter upon some new engagement; or sit down to write a letter; or start on a journey; or prepare to meet a friend. To the man of whom we spoke at the beginning of this chapter, the kitchen was as holy a place as a church. All his work was wrought in God. Daily he had sweet talk with Him, as he went about his humble service. He began every part of his duties with silent prayer. As the work went forward, he would lift up his heart again in prayer; and when it was finished, he would give thanks for help received, or confess the sin of his failure. Thus the fireside, with its pots and pans, its heat and smells, became like the gate of heaven to him; and his soul was as much united to God

amid the tasks of the kitchen, as when he was in his private room.

By practice, remembering God as much as we can, and asking Him to forgive when we had passed long hours in forgetfulness of Him, this habit would become **easy** and natural to us —a kind of second nature.

(3) Then again, we might do much to fix this habit, by cultivating the practice of talking to God aloud, as we would to a friend, in the most natural way, and about the most trivial incidents of life. How much they miss, who only speak to God from their knees, or on set occasions! There must be such times for us all; but we may link them together by a perpetual ripple of holy and loving converse with Him, who counts the hairs of our heads in His minute microscopic interest in our concerns.

It was surely thus that Enoch walked with God. And it was this which enabled Bishop Taylor to say, "I am a witness to the fact that the Lord Jesus is alive; that He is a person; and though invisible, accessible. I have been cultivating personal acquaintance with a personal Saviour for more than forty-three years."

There are special times when we may fall back with an emphasis of comfort on this majestic consciousness. In prayer, Psalm cxlv. 18; in deep sorrow for sin, Isaiah l. 8; in anguish of grief, Psalm xxxiv. 18; in hours of perplexity, Luke xxiv. 15; in days of peril, 2 Kings vi. 16; in the approach of temptation, Psalm cxix. 151, 152.

And we may ever count upon the ready help of the Holy Ghost, whose mission is to remind us of what we should otherwise forget, and to make to us what, through the imperfection of our nature, might become blurred and indistinct. This at least may be our comfort, in these days of our pilgrimage, that His presence is ever going with us, as it went with Moses; and that presence is manna and water, guidance and protection, deliverance and rest. "In Thy presence is fulness of joy. At Thy right hand there are pleasures forevermore."

"I AM WITH YOU ALL THE DAYS."

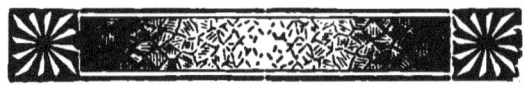

II.
"My Peace I Give."
John xiv. 27.

THESE words from such lips, and at such a time, were something more than a common Eastern salutation. They contained Christ's parting benediction to those whom He loved better than His life. And at the moment of speaking, He did forever allot to His beloved disciples, and to the believers of all time, a legacy of Peace, such as filled His own breast with unruffled calm. They might not realize all that His word involved; but their failure did not annul the wealth or glory of the bequest.

Forgiveness.

And, as the years passed on, they only revealed more and more of the depths of meaning which lay concealed in these unfathomable words.

We should carefully accentuate that pronoun, "My." It is not so much of the Peace that He purchased with His blood, nor of the Peace of heaven—that our Saviour here speaks: but of the very peace that filled His own glorious nature, and kept it so calm and still amid the storms that swept around His pathway through the world. This Peace He waits to give. Standing beside some reader of these lines—who, it may be, is careworn and anxious, the head aching with anxious thought, the heart sick, and the brow furrowed with deep lines of care—He speaks and says, "My peace I give unto thee." Let us take Him at His word, and appropriate the gift with rejoicing faith.

If we now turn to John xx. 19, 21,

26, with its threefold benediction of peace, we may be able to distinguish some three further shades of meaning in the peace which Jesus offers.

I. There is, First, The Peace of Forgiveness (19th verse).

This is the peace of the Evening. When the day is done, with its rush of business and care, its multitudinous demands on heart, and head, and hands, what a relief it is to shut the doors, to exclude all intruders, and to meet with beloved and familiar faces! And yet, even at such times, there are thoughts which we cannot exclude. The disciples might shut the doors of the upper chamber, for fear of the Jews; but those doors could not exclude the memory of their late unfaithfulness and cowardice, their treachery and desertion. And these bitter thoughts were more terrible to endure than their fear of hostile intruders. Such is often our own experience. The day that opened so bright and fair has become marred by many sad and painful incidents, which we have been able to disregard amid the impetuous rush of life, but which refuse to be longer ignored, and return to oppress and sadden our hearts, like a recurring nightmare, as we sit down to rest in the quiet of our own chambers, beneath the fall of night.

Some impatience or outburst of irritability; an unkind word; a look of annoyance; a selfish preference of ourselves to others whom we really love; some indulgence, however momentary, of evil imagination and unholy desire; some acts of meanness or overreaching in our business. Ah, it all comes back to us afresh! What would we not give not to have yielded so weakly; or to be able to live the time over again! But, alas! it is beyond recall. And our only comfort is in the presence of the Peace-giver, who, standing beside us, says gently, "My peace I give unto you;" and shows us His hands and His side, marked still by the wound-prints of Calvary, the pledge and guarantee of forgiveness through His blood. At such times let us gratefully accept what He brings; and wrap ourselves about in the mantle of His tender, forgiving grace, as the dark brown earth of winter wraps itself in the mantle of soft, white snow.

The great enemy of peace is the consciousness of sin. He who would give us peace must deal with that first. And our Saviour is equal to the task, coming fresh from Calvary, "a Lamb as it had been slain:" revealing the warrant and ground of Justification; so that we may say with the Apostle, "Being justified by faith, we have peace with God;" and may lay down to sleep with the Angels of peace and forgiveness watching us through the hours of unconsciousness.

II. There is, next, Peace in Service (21st verse).

This is the Peace of the MORNING. We should never leave our room until we have seen the face of our dear Master, Christ, and have realized that we are being sent forth by Him to do His will, and to finish the work which He has given us to do. He who said to His immediate followers, "As My Father hath sent Me, even so I send you," says as much to each one of us, as the dawn summons us to live another day. We should realize that we are as much sent forth by Him as the angels who "do His commandments, hearkening unto the voice of His word." There is some plan for each day's work, which He will unfold to us, if only we will look up to Him to do so; some mission to fulfill; some ministry to perform; some irksome task to do better for His sake; some lesson patiently to learn, that we may be able "to teach others also."

Is it not very helpful to hear Him say, morning by morning, as He reveals His plan, and gives His strength, and sends us forth, "My peace I give unto thee!" And that Peace the world cannot take away. Amid its wildest alarms and tumults "the peace of God, that passeth all understanding," *sentinels* the heart and mind. "In the world ye shall have tribulation: these things I have spoken unto you that in Me ye might have peace."

Our peace is often broken by the demands of service, and in two directions. On the one hand, we do not exactly know *what to do*; and on the other, we are doubtful as to whether we have *adequate strength* for the fulfilment of the task set us. But each of these breakers of peace can be met and silenced by the words before us. As to our plans we need not be anxious; because He who sends us forth is responsible to make the plan, according to His infinite wisdom; and to reveal it to us, however dull and stupid our faculties may be. And as to our sufficiency, we are secure of having all needful grace; because He never sends us forth, except He first breathes on us and says, "Receive ye the Holy Ghost." There is always a special endowment for special power. The breath is so gentle and light, that we are often ignorant of it; it passes as the zephyr over the flowers and is gone. But it is not withheld from any true heart, who is eager to do Christ's work on Christ's plan, and in His strength.

III. THERE IS, LASTLY, PEACE IN SORROW (26th verse).

This is the peace of DARK HOURS.

Such sorrow has seldom darkened human hearts as that which settled on these men, and especially on Thomas. The agony of his doubt was in proportion to the strength and tenderness of His love (John xi. 16.) He could not believe. And sometimes we have passed through phases of experience which have enabled us to understand the bitterness of his soul. When a whole storehouse of blessings has awaited our turning the key of faith in the golden lock, but we seem to have utterly lost it, and can only lie helpless at the feet of Christ, bemoaning our inability to believe—at such times Jesus comes to us, and stands beside us, within reach ("Reach hither," John xx. 27,) if not within sight ("have not seen," verse 29.) He suits Himself to our need; and stoops to fulfill our conditions; and tenderly lifts up the bruised and broken soul; whispering as He does so, "My peace I give unto thee."

Peace in Sorrow.

Dark hours come to us all; and if we have no clue to a peace that can pass unbroken through their murky gloom, we shall be in a state of continual dread. Any stone flung by a chance passer-by may break the crystal clearness of the Lake of Peace, and send disturbing ripples across it, unless we have learnt to trust in the perpetual presence of Him who can make and keep a "great calm" within the soul.

Only let nothing come to you, which you shall not instantly hand over to Him; all petty worries; all crushing difficulties; all inability to believe. Tell them all to Him, "who knows all, and loves us better than He knows." And, in response, He will hush our troubled heart, and drive away its fears, lulling us as a mother soothes her babe. "Let not your heart be troubled, neither let it be afraid. Peace I leave with you; My peace I give unto you."

III.
"Cleanseth."
1 John i. 7.

ONE of the most precious chapters in the New Testament tells us that on the eve of His departure to His Father, while His heart was brimming with high thoughts of His origin and destiny, our Lord Jesus left the lowly meal, and girded Himself with a towel, and began to wash the feet of His disciples. (John xiii.) He refused to do more than this when Peter asked Him; because He said that those who had recently bathed, needed to do no more than cleanse their feet; which, after the Eastern fashion, were unprotected, save by open sandals, from the dust and grit of the roads. He washed their feet therefore, and they were clean, EVERY WHIT.

This incident, in which Divine Majesty shone forth in Divine humility, is not only a part of the Gospel, a story of eighteen hundred years ago; it is a fact of the living present. Judged by the Divine arithmetic, which reckons a thousand years as one day, it only happened on the evening of the day before yesterday. Judged by the reckoning of faith, it is taking place to-day.

There are two ways of reading the narratives of the Gospels. We may study them, with adoring wonder, as the story of what Christ was; or we may look up from each verse to Him, and feel it to be the record of what He is. Each view is right; and we need to blend them: but, as a matter of fact, we more often look on the evangelists as historians of the past, than as chroniclers of the present. We forget that Jesus Christ is the same to-day, when He is sitting on the throne, as He was yesterday, when He trod the pathway of our world. And in this forgetfulness how much we miss! What He was, that He is. What He said, that He says. The Gospels are simply specimens of the life that He is ever living; they are leaves torn out of the diary of His unchangeable Being.

To-day He is sitting on the Mountains of Beatitudes to teach, whilst all nature, like an open book, lies before His eye to give Him parables that shall make the eyes of children glisten, whilst they instruct the most profound. To-day He is working miracles of healing on the crowds of suffering ones; passing down infirmary wards, visiting fever-houses, standing in sick rooms, with His *Talitha cumi*, and His healing touch. To-day He rides in lowly triumph, amid the love of troops of children and of loyal friends, while the Pharisees and Sadducees mock Him to scorn. To-day, also, He is engaged in washing the feet of His disciples, soiled with their wilderness journeyings. Yes, that charming incident is having its fulfillment in thee, my friend, if only thou dost not refuse the lowly loving offices of Him whom we call Master and Lord, but who still girds Himself and comes forth to serve.

And we *must* have this incessant cleansing if we would keep right. It is not enough to look back to a certain hour when we first knelt at the feet of the Son of God for pardon; and heard Him say, "Thy sins, which are many, are all forgiven." We need daily, hourly, cleansing—from daily, hourly sin.

Learn a lesson from the eye of the miner, who all day long is working amid the flying coal-dust. When he emerges in the light of day, his face may be grimy enough; but his eyes are clear and lustrous, because the fountain of tears, in the lachrymal gland, is ever pouring its gentle tides over the eye, cleansing away each speck of dust as soon as it alights. Is not this the miracle of cleansing which our spirits need in such a world as this? And this is what our blessed Lord is prepared to do for us, if only we will trust Him.

The Blood of Jesus is always speaking for us before the throne of God. It was sprinkled there for us by our great High Priest, when He entered as our forerunner; and its presence there is our only plea for mercy. But that same Blood is ever needed by us for the purposes of inward purity. It is not enough to quote it, in the past tense, as "having cleansed." We need to quote it in a perpetual present; and to say, *it cleanseth*. Whenever you shudder at the evil of your old nature asserting itself, in some hideous thought or desire, look up and claim the cleansing of the precious Blood.

Whenever you are assailed by the tempter who, as he knocks at the door of your soul, soils the clean doorstep with his tread, look up again, and claim the office of your Saviour, to efface each footprint, and to remove each stain.

Whenever you are horrified in contemplating the immense distance between your best and the ideal manhood of Jesus, and the sense of shortcomings appals your soul, there is but one resort that can avail you; it is not the brazen altar, where the sacrifice was slain, but the laver where the priests may wash as often as they need.

Whenever you have been betrayed into sudden sin, do not wait till the evening, or for a more convenient time and place; but there, just where you are, lift up your heart to your compassionate Saviour, and ask Him to wash you and make you whiter than snow.

Before entering the House of God; before participating in any act of service; before undertaking any work of ministry—it is our bounden duty to seek the cleansing away of all that may have stained our raiment, and fouled our hearts. In all quiet moments it becomes us to consider our need of washing our feet. If we lived thus, we should find that our communion would be unbroken; and that the Great Master would constantly take us in His hands to employ us in His work. What Jesus wants is not gold or silver vessels, but *clean* ones. And though a vessel be earthenware, if only it is clean, He will use it; whilst He will pass by the one of chastest pattern, which is impure, or difficult to handle.

It is impossible to exaggerate the

importance of these words. Lie as a stone in the bed of the cleansing grace of Christ; no impurities can penetrate thither. Remove each drop of acid as it alights on the burnished steel. And let this present tense become the watchword of a Blessed Life: "THE BLOOD OF JESUS CHRIST, HIS SON, CLEANSETH ME FROM ALL SIN."

IV.
"Worketh."
John v. 17.

GOD is the great Worker in the World. Though He entered into His rest on the seventh day, yet His rest has been full of work. He works in rest, and rests in work. The operations of Nature, the course of Providence, and the evolution of an evident plan in history; all these are living tokens of His unwearying activity. "Of Him, and through Him, and to Him, are all things; to whom be glory forever."

We must be very careful not to hide this fact of God's personal activity under the veil of the Reign of Law. Men speak much of Law, as if they considered that laws were forces; when, in point of fact, a law is simply the unvarying method in which the force works which is behind it, mysterious and ineffable. Talk of Law, and you have explained nothing as to the essence of the force itself. And if you demand what that force is, there is but one reply, adequate to the enquiry; and it is given in the one all-containing word—GOD.

God's workshop is the Universe; but you may also find it in the surrendered heart. There is a beautiful illustration of this in the life of our Lord. When His enemies found fault with Him for having healed the paralytic man on the Sabbath day, He answered, "My Father worketh hitherto, and I work." This deep answer to the question is not always understood or appreciated. The usual explanation is, that deeds of mercy no more broke the Sabbath than the incessant workings of God interfered with His rest. But there is something still deeper. The in-workings and promptings of the Father had been stirring within our Saviour's spirit, even up to that moment, and to that miracle; and therefore He, as the Servant and Son, had no alternative than to obey. If then they found fault at all, it should not be with Himself, but with that energising Will, which had moved Him to the act that had aroused their hate.

Now, in a lesser degree, but on the same lines, God works in all loving and obedient hearts; so that the Apostle could say, "Work out your own salvation with fear and trembling! for it is God *that worketh in you* both to will and to do of His good pleasure." (Phil. ii. 12, 13.) The same truth appears in many other places. "His working,which worketh in me mightily." "Working in you that which is well-pleasing in His sight."

What a weight of staggering thought is excited by these words! Stay, my soul, and wonder, that the Eternal God should stoop to work within thy narrow limits—filthy as a stable; dark as a cellar; stifling as an over-crowded room. Is it not a marvel indeed, that He, whom the heavens cannot contain, and in whose sight they are not clean, should trouble Himself to work on material so unpromising, and amidst circumstances so uncongenial? How careful should we be to make Him welcome, and to throw no hindrance in His way! how eager to garner up all the least movements of His gracious operation—as the machinist conserves the force of his engine; and as the goldsmith, with miserly care, collects every flake of gold-leaf! Surely we shall be sensible of the *fear* of holy reverence and the *trembling* of eager anxiety; as we "work out," into daily act and life, all that God our Father is "working in."

Of course, in one sense our salvation is complete; but in another it is still in process. "We are being saved." We were saved from the condemnation and penalty of sin, when Jesus died; we are being saved from indwelling sin, through the gracious renewal of the Holy Ghost; and we shall yet be saved, so far as the emancipation of the body is concerned, when the trumpet of the archangel has given the signal of Resurrection. It is of the middle term in this series, that we are thinking now; of that salvation which consists in delivering us from the power of indwelling sin, and in fashioning us into the likeness of the Son of God.

The agent in this work is God Himself. He dwells in the surrendered heart; and He drives all evil before him, as the first beams of light expelled the brooding chaos from the universe. But He does not perform His work mechanically, irresistibly, or by iron force.

He works by promptings, movings, checkings, suggestions, inspirations, touches light as a feather and soft as an angel's. If we treat these workings with neglect, they subside; and the soul resembles one of those deserted pits, in which the machinery and *debris* tell of the busy tides of workmen that have long since ebbed away. If, on the other hand, we carefully obey them, they become more powerful; and our obedience makes their effect permanent in our characters. *Obedience to a divine prompting transforms it into a permanent acquisition.* It is a new piece of workmanship, whether of gold, silver, or precious stones, built into the fabric of the spiritual nature.

There is one important matter, however, which we must bear carefully in mind. If we attend only to the inner working and striving of God's Holy Spirit, we may become confused as to what is really His; for Satan will simulate it, that he may annoy us, transforming himself into an angel of light. We should therefore remember that God educates human spirits by three agencies: by the Word, by the Spirit, and by the events of Providence. And these three always agree in one; they never clash. Whensoever, therefore, we are sensible of a mighty striving within our hearts, we should test it by the Word of God on the one hand; and on the other we should await the opening of circumstances. If we follow the inner light without the Bible, we shall become visionaries. If we follow the inner light without awaiting the unfolding of circumstances, we shall be unpractical.

Let it be our chosen attitude to

open our whole being increasingly to the inworking of God. We were originally "His workmanship, created unto good works." And now, let us ask Him to work in us to WILL those good works, so that our WILL, without being impaired in its free operation, may be permeated and moulded by His will; just as light suffuses the atmosphere, without displacing it. And let us also expect that He will infuse into us sufficient strength that we may be able to *do* His will unto all pleasing. Thus, day by day, our life will be a manifestation of those holy volitions, and lovely deeds, which shall attest the indwelling and inworking of God. And men shall see our good works, and glorify our Father which is in Heaven.

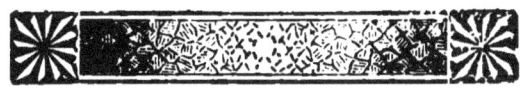

V.
"Strengtheneth."
PHILIPPIANS iv. 13.

IT was a marvellous statement for a man to make: "I can do all things." At first sight we suppose the speaker had either had but very little experience of the world with its varying conditions; or that he was some favoured child of fortune, who had never known want, because possessing an abundant supply of wealth and power.

But closer consideration removes each supposition; and we find ourselves face to face with a prisoner bound to a Roman soldier, who had run through the whole scale of human experience, now touching its abundant fulness, and anon descending to its most abject want; one who said himself: "I know how to be abased, and I know also how to abound; in everything and in all things have I learned the secret both to be filled and to be hungry, both to abound and to be in want." It was, therefore, after a very profound experience of the extremes of human life, and of all the variations between, that the Apostle made that confident assertion: "I can do all things."

It is a temper of mind which we might well covet. To be superior to every need; to bear prosperity without pride, and adversity without a murmur; to feel that there is no earthly circumstance that can disturb the soul from its equilibrium in God; to be able to yoke the most untamable difficulties to the car of spiritual progress; to have such a sense of power as to laugh at impossibility and to sing in adversity; to help the weak, even though we might seem to need every scrap of power for ourselves; to feel amid the changing conditions of life as a strong swimmer does in the midst of the ocean waves, which he beats back in the proud consciousness of power—all this, and much more, is involved in the expression, "I can do all things."

And when we ask for the talisman, which has given a frail man this marvellous power, it is given in the words: *"in him that strengtheneth Me."* The Old Version gave *through Christ;* the New alters it to *"In Him."* And at once we see the connection with all that line of inner teaching, of which, to the careful student, the Bible is so full. Those words are the keynote of Blessedness, first struck by our Lord, and repeated with unwearying persistence by His immediate followers, to whom they were the secret of an overcoming life. The one main thought of them is this—that the strength that we covet, is not given to us in a lump, for us to draw upon as we choose, like electricity stored in boxes for use; it is a life, and it is only to be obtained so long as we are in living union with its source. Apart from Him we can do nothing. Whilst we are abiding in Him, nothing is impossible. The one purpose of our life should therefore be to remain in living and intense union with Christ, guarding against everything that would break it, employing every means of cementing and enlarging it. And just in proportion as we do so, we shall find His strength flowing into us for every possible emergency. We may not feel its presence; but we shall find it present whenever we begin to draw on it. Or if ever we are more than usually sensible of our weakness, one moment of upward looking will be sufficient to bring it in a tidal wave of fulness into our hearts.

There is no temptation which we cannot master; no privation which we cannot patiently bear; no difficulty with which we cannot cope; no work which we cannot perform; no confession or testimony which we cannot make—if only our souls are living in healthy union with Jesus Christ, for as our day, or hour, is, so shall our strength be: so much so, that we shall be perfectly surprised at ourselves, as we look back on what we have accomplished.

Dwell on the present tense, *Strengtheneth.* Hour by hour, as the tides of the golden sun-heat are quietly absorbed by flowers and giant trees—so will the strength of the living Saviour pass into our receptive natures. He will stand by us; He will dwell in us; He will live through us—strengthening us with strength in our souls.

The dying patriarch told how his favourite child would be made strong, by the mighty God of Jacob putting His Almighty hands over his trembling fingers; as an archer might lay his brawny skilled hands on the delicate grasp of his child, teaching him how to point the arrow, and enabling him to pull back the bow string. Oh what beauty there is in the comparison! Who would not wish to be such a favoured one, feeling ever the gentle touch of the hands of God, empowering us, and working with us! Yet that portion may be thine, dear reader, and mine. To the prayer first offered by Nehemiah—"O God, strengthen my hand," God answers Himself: "I will strengthen thee." "Wait on the Lord, and He shall strengthen thine heart." "They that wait upon the Lord shall change their strength," *i. e.* they shall exchange one degree of strength for another, in an ever ascending scale. The strength of Christ is never found in the heart that boasts its own strength. The two can no more coexist, than light and darkness can coexist in the same space. And therefore the Apostle used to glory in any thing that reminded him of his utter helplessness and weakness. This thought made him even acquiesce willingly to the thorn in his flesh. It was at first his repeated prayer that it might be removed; but when the Lord explained that His strength could only be perfected in weakness, and that the presence of the thorn was a perpetual indication and reminder of the weakness of his flesh, driving him to the Strong for strength, and making him a fit subject for the conspicuous manifestations of God's might at its full— then he protested that he would most gladly glory in his weakness, that the strength of Christ might rest upon him; for when he was

Difficulties and Trials.

weak, in his own deep consciousness, then he was strong in the strength of the strong Son of God. (2 Cor. xii. 9.)

It would be a great help to us all if we could look at difficulties and trials in this way. Considering that they have been sent, not to grieve or annoy us, but to make us despair of ourselves, and to force us to make use of that divine storehouse of power, which is so close to us, but of which we make so little use. Difficulties are God's way of leading us to rely on His almighty sufficiency. They are none of them insurmountable; they are the triumphs of His art; they are meant to reveal to us resources of which, had it not been for their compulsion, we might have lived in perpetual ignorance—just as hunger has led to many of the most wonderful inventions.

What glorious lives might be the lot of the readers of these lines, if only they would abjure their own strength—be it wisdom, wealth, station, or any other source of creature aid; and if they would learn that the true strength is to sit still at the source of all might and grace, receiving out of His fulness, and mingling the song of the psalm, with the glad affirmation of the Apostle: "I will love Thee, O Lord, my strength;" "I can do all things through Christ that strengtheneth me!"

VI.
"Liveth."
Revelation ix-18.

LIFE is triumphant! That is the glad witness of the New Testament, and especially of the Apocalypse. It was a revelation indeed to the world, on which it broke, as tidings of great joy. Up to that moment, the majority of men, including some of the foremost of the race, had thought that death, and night, and chaos, would end all.

And some of the sublimest conceptions of the ancient world embody this sad foreboding for all time—the Prometheus, in which man struggles heroically but hopelessly, whilst the eagle of irresistible destiny feeds upon his vitals; or the Laocoon, in which man, in his sinewy strength is involved with slender youth, in the coils of the serpents of fate, against which they struggle in vain. Children were born to die. Flowers bloomed to fade. The glory of the spring smiled but for a transient hour, amid the marble of their temples and beside the deep azure of their ocean waves. All things at last seemed doomed to be overcome by the dark elements, which waged perpetual war against life, and beauty, and joy.

Into the midst of such a world the tidings came that Life was the mightier force; and that Life was victor.

And when men asked the reason for an assertion so confident and so glad, the answer was given in some such terms as these:—"There lived in Palestine One, who, during His brief life, was the assailant of death in all its varied forms. He beat back, by His touch and word, its approach. He compelled it to lay down the young life which it had only just taken up. He brought from the grave those who had long passed from the bourne of the living world. And yet, though He might have seemed impervious to death, at last He too succumbed to its power; and the brightest hopes that had ever been born in human hearts seemed destined to hopeless destruction. But it was only for an instant. Three days were long enough to show that He could not be holden by death. He broke from its prison-house, and came forth victor over its supremest efforts. He made Himself known to His friends as the Living One; speaking and talking to them as of old. And to the purged eye of him whom He loved He gave one last glorious vision of Himself in the sea-girt isle of Patmos, saying, as He did so: "Fear not; I am the first and the last, and THE LIVING ONE; and I was dead, and behold I am alive for evermore, and I have the keys of death and of Hades." (Rev. i. 18, R. V.)

This was the keynote of the gladness of the early Church: "We know that our Redeemer liveth." And as the centuries have slowly rolled away, they have not been able to rob the Church of her faith. Year after year she has celebrated Easter with songs. And in the darkest time she has saluted the living Saviour with the words: "When Thou hadst overcome the sharpness of death, Thou didst open the Kingdom of Heaven to all believers."

Who can fathom all the consolation which we enjoy, and which is due to the fact that our Lord Jesus is living in an eternal present, never more to see corruption?

He lives as our High Priest. There was a fatal defect in the Jewish priesthood, because they were not able to continue, by reason of death. As soon as a High Priest became thoroughly versed in his duties, and familiar with his charge, he had to follow the steps of his great predecessor, who died on the summit of Mount Hor. But *this Man*, because He continueth ever, hath an unchangeable Priesthood. "Wherefore also He is able to save to the uttermost them that draw near unto God through Him, seeing He ever liveth." What music is in those words! When we come to God, it is by a *living* way. Nor should we be content to leave our morning or evening prayer, till we have had living contact with the Living One Himself. Prayer may be a law; but it is equally a direct converse with a real living personal friend—the Prince who is our Brother —the King who is of near kin to us. And this is surely the happy experience of the Blessed Life. To know that there is no cloud between Him and the soul; and to repeat again and again vows of loyalty and devotion, spoken not into the responseless air, but into the living ear of One whose heart responds in unutterable tenderness to the stillest whisper of affection and trust.

He lives as the Source of our Life. "Because I live, ye shall live also." This teaching was borrowed from His own deep inner life. His life, in a very significant sense, was not His own; it was His Father's. He said that the words He spoke, and the works He did, were not His, but were the outcome of His Father's indwelling. "The living Father hath sent Me, and I live by the Father." Thus it happened, that all who saw Him, saw His Father; and His life has been, for all the ages, a manifestation of the unseen God.

Similarly, for us who have believed, and, in believing, have received the germ of eternal life, He is willing to be all that His Father was to Him.

He is our life. To us to live is Christ. The Son of God liveth in us. The life of Jesus is manifest in our mortal flesh. As, in the olden vision, the precious oil came through the golden pipes to feed the temple-lamp, so does His life come through our faith to feed our spirits.

Happy are they who are dead to their own life; who steadily ignore it and deny it—that the life of Jesus may have free scope in them to rise up into all the beauty and glory of perfect life! With Him is the fountain of life; would that all our fresh springs were ever consciously also in Him! We do not need to concern ourselves about the progress of His life within us, if only we are careful to mortify that other life, *our own;* and to obey all the throbbings and promptings of His life which is ever pining for fuller manifestation within us. Give yourself wholly up to Him, that He may live through your being, until He shall even quicken your mortal body, and raise it up in resurrection-glory.

He lives to lead on the Ages to all the Possibilities of Life. What lies before us we cannot tell—what glory, what radiant bliss, what rapture! We only know that He spake, not only of life, but of life "more abundantly." And we are told that He will lead us "Unto fountains of waters of life." George Fox tells of his dream, in which he saw the ocean of life sweep away the inky waters of death forever; but who shall fathom that ocean, or tell its expanse, its depth, its shores?

This is at least true—that He will never rest until He has enlarged our capacities to comprehend, and our hearts to receive, the fulness of His life. We are only learning its alphabet. We are like a brood just out of the egg, lying close in the nest, taking only what is given us, and utterly

The Fulness of His Life.

ignorant of the undeveloped powers of flight, which shall enable us to flash in the sunny air. But the time is coming when we shall drink of His life, and live for ever with Himself.

Till then let us eat of His flesh, in rapt meditation on His words; and let us drink of His blood, in loving communion with His sacrifice and death; that so we may have His life abiding in us, and in the most emphatic sense may live by Him, until mortality shall be swallowed up of life. And of this let us be sure, that our spiritual life, though tried and tested, can never be extinguished, because it is guaranteed by One who

"EVER LIVETH."

VII.
"Loveth."
REV. I. 5.

WHAT a wealth of meaning is brought out by the Revised Translation of the Doxology, caught from the minstrelsy of Heaven, with which the Apostle John opens the book of Revelation! We have been accustomed to read, "Unto Him that loved us;" but we now find it translated from the past tense to the present, " Unto Him that LOVETH us." The love of Jesus to His own is an eternal noon; a perpetual present; an ocean fulness without tide or shadow of turning

Of course, He loved us, and bore us on His heart, before the worlds were made. It was for love of us that He emptied Himself, and became obedient to the death of the Cross. Yes, and He will love us, with the love of the Bridegroom towards the Bride, through those golden ages which we are to spend with Him, dating from the marriage feast, and ending never. But this is the most priceless thought of all—that He loves us NOW. If He loved me when He gave Himself for me, it is certain that He loves me equally to-day; because He is the same in the to-day of the present, as He was in the yesterday of the past, and as He will be in the for-ever of the future. He is always "this same Jesus." (Acts i. 11.) Time, which changes all things else, is foiled when it approaches the heart of Christ. The flight of ages cannot lessen, or chill, or affect His Love. "This Man because He continueth ever hath an unchangeable priesthood".

"Loveth."

We are so apt to judge of the Love of Christ to us by our appreciation and enjoyment of it. It is easy to believe in it when we are bright in spirits and well in health; when the atmosphere is clear, and the air is invigorating, and the sun shines brightly; or when we are living in happy obedience, and conscious fellowship. It needs no great effort, under such circumstances, to be sure of the Love of Christ. But when our sky is overcast, and our way lies through a tangled jungle; when they are increased that trouble us, and misfortunes tread on each other's heels; when we are conscious of failure and sin—it is not natural to us then to calculate on the unchanged love of Christ. Yet we might as well suppose that the heat given out by the sun varied with the temperature of our fickle northern climate, as think that the Love of Christ changes with every variation in ourselves. It is a constant quantity. It is not turned away by our sins. It is not lessened by our coldness or neglect. Like some perennial spring, it cannot be bound by frost, or reduced by drought, or exhausted by the demands of generations.

The truant servant, lying spiritless on the desert sands; the headstrong apostle venting denials and oaths in the midst of the servants of his Master's foes; the back-slider, reaping the bitter harvest of his ways; the discouraged exile, mourning in the land of the Hermonites over the happy past—all these may look up to the empyrean of the love of Christ, and be sure that He loveth with a constant and unwavering attachment. Write this on the tablets of your heart, reader; that neither sin, nor depression, nor height, nor depth, nor things present, nor things to come, shall be able to alter the fulness and constancy of the love of Christ to you. If only Christians would really grasp this great truth, and would dare, in frequent contradiction to their own feelings, to believe in and affirm the unchanging love of God, they would reach a firm standing ground from which the great adversary of souls could never dislodge them.

"I am feeling loneless and depressed; but God loves me!" "I am groping my way through the darkness; but God loves me!" "I have fallen, and am no better than others; but God loves me!" "I am passing through a season of sore chastening; but this makes me only more sure that my Father loveth me!" This is the secret of victory and rest.

Our Lord bade us abide in His love. "If ye keep my commandments, ye shall abide in My love; even as I have kept My Father's commandments, and abide in His love"—of course, this means in the consciousness of His love. It is one thing to be in the light, and quite another thing to know it. There is a sense in which we are all living in the light of Christ's love; but we do not all enjoy it as a living practical experience. "Keep yourselves in the love of God. *i. e.*, cultivate an habitual consciousness of the love of God toward you.

There are seven golden rules for acquiring and maintaining this consciousness.

(1) Never leave your room in the morning without a distinct apprehension of the fact that "the Father Himself loveth you." (John xvi. 27.)

(2) Ask the Holy Spirit—who sheds abroad the love of God in the heart, and who brings all things to our remembrance—that you may hear the whispers of His still, small voice, perpetually reminding you that God loves you.

(3) Accept all lovely things—gentle words; kindly acts; gleams of sunlight; the songs of birds and the scent of flowers—as being the token of His love; and look up with a smile to Him, as you say, "I thank Thee."

(4) Avoid all things that are inconsistent with the fact of your being God's beloved child; all irritableness and fretfulness; all petulance and anger; all ill-speaking, and uncharitableness.

(5) Do the meanest and most trivial things for the love of God, as one constrained by that love not to live to self, but to Him; and let your one aim be to do all things as one whom God loves.

(6) Let no commandment, of which you are aware, lie on the page of Scripture unobeyed. "He that hath My commandments and keepeth them he it is that loveth Me; and he that loveth Me shall be loved of My Father; and I will love him, and will

manifest Myself to him." (John xiv. 21.)

(7) Cultivate a spirit of disinterested love and kindness to all. "He that dwelleth in Love, dwelleth in God, and God in him."

Rooted and grounded in love to others, we comprehend best the love of God to ourselves.

It was the charm of our Saviour's life, that He was able to say, *the Father loveth the Son.* (John v. 20.)

Unloved and unwelcomed by those whom He came to save, He found solace and a home in the unchanging love of God. On the eve of His death, He could wish for us nothing better than that we should enjoy the love wherewith the Father had loved Him.

Let us not miss our heritage by supineness or neglect. But let us live, as He did, beneath the spell of this sweet and heart-stirring strain—

"HE LOVETH US."

VIII.
"Reigneth."
REV. xix. 6.

WHAT a mirror of human life and history is the Book of the Revelation! One seems to be standing in a great battlefield; all around armed legions break in battle-shock; shining legions locked in deadly conflict with the dark hosts of hell; the cries of the down-trodden, the dying, and the martyred victims wail aloud upon the breeze: but amid all the din and tumult, ever and again rise up the sweet, clear-voiced choruses of redeemed and victorious ones, who cheer the fainting and rally the desponding, and hail the growing symptoms of Heaven's ultimate victory. Such a chorus

The Song of Victory.

rings out upon our ear and heart in the words before us (Rev. xix. 6).

The previous chapters are full of agony and conflict; the ploughshare of war is driven through the world; and the Apostate Church meets her doom. As a millstone might be dashed by a strong angel into the ocean, so is Babylon thrown down, never to be found any more. And as she sinks down to her doom, there is heard a great voice of much people in heaven, saying, "Alleluia!" And again they say, "Alleluia!" And yet again the four-and-twenty elders and the four living creatures say, "Amen, Alleluia!" And then there issues once more a solitary voice from out of the throne, calling for yet further praise; and in response, the Apostle John tells us, "I heard as it were the voice of a great multitude, and as the voice of mighty thunderings, saying, "Alleluia; for the Lord God Omnipotent reigneth!"

Yes, there is always a Hallelujah Chorus, whenever the Lord reigns. We shall join in *that* song of victory and triumph ere long. Every sunrise brings it nearer. But we need not wait for the establishment of the millennial kingdom, ere we hear or raise the ringing cry of "Hallelujah!" We may catch it ringing even now around the earth; we may hear it breaking gladly from redeemed heart, and surrendered lives, which have learnt that the reign of Jesus is always associated with the Hallelujah Chorus.

Even the Old Testament teaches this, in three memorable Psalms, lying almost on the same page—xciii., xcvii., xcix. The first teaches His Kingdom *over Nature*. We hear the break of the waves, the mighty waves of the sea, lifting up their voices. But the Lord on high is mightier than the mightiest. "The Lord reigneth; Hallelujah!"

The second teaches His kingdom *over men*. His enemies, and Judah's daughters, alike own His sway. The most careless and rebellious are subservient to His designs. "He doeth according to His will in the army of Heaven and among the inhabitants of the earth." Men plot and scheme as they will; but they only do what His hand, or His counsel, determined before to be done. And as we consider the reality of the glory of His sway—not less a fact because unrealizied by its subjects—we again cry: "The Lord reigneth; Hallelujah!"

The third teaches us that His kingdom is *over saints*. "The Lord is great in Zion." The saints recognize but one supreme headship of the Church; and as they look up to Him who is guiding her course, and governing her politics, unaffected by the apparent contrarieties and disunion amongst us, again they cry, "The Lord reigneth; Hallelujah!"

But surely all this applies most closely to our own individual experience. We never knew what true joy was until the meek and lowly Saviour rode in triumph as King over our hearts. But before that moment we had been distracted with riot and revolt; with bitter experiences of failure and disappointment; with a weary sense of an anarchy, which we could not put down. But when He entered to set up His reign, the cry of "Hosannah!" rang through the citadel of our inner being; and it seemed as if angel-voices sang to us, "Rejoice greatly! fear not, for thy King cometh!"

Ah! the devil's lie has been but too successful in leading men to think that Christ's reign means misery and privation. It is because they have believed it that so many have excluded themselves from it altogether; or have submitted only a part of their being to his blessed empire, giving Him the environs, whilst they reserve the citadel, the Zion, for themselves. But those who know what it is to yield their whole being to His government, know that where there is the increase of His government, there is also the increase of peace, and of each there need be no end (Isaiah ix. 7.)

Would that some who have been living a sad and bitter life, might haul down the flag of revolt, and welcome the King whose reign is founded on His priesthood, the true Melchizedek, the Priest-king; and as the King of Glory passes the uplifted gates, and His standard flies from the citadel of the will, there shall ring out the cry, "Hallelujah! the Lord God omnipotent reigneth."

You have only to open the gates to Him, and He will subdue all authority and power; He will bring every thought into captivity; He will keep down the rebellious nature.

Remember He is omnipotent—omnipotent to conquer; omnipotent to keep; omnipotent to reign. Life then shall become one long Hallelujah, growing deeper and sweeter as the years roll on. No event will disturb or perplex, because in each incident we shall see the result of our king's appointment; and whether we like it or not, whether it causes us pain or joy, whether it shine or showers, we shall be able to cry,

"HALLELUJAH!
FOR THE LORD GOD OMNIPOTENT
REIGNETH."

IX.
"Teacheth."
1 JOHN ii. 27.

THAT was a true word spoken by the prophet when he said, "All thy children shall be taught of the Lord; and great shall be the peace of thy children." (Isaiah liv. 13.) It is certain that the amount of peace which we enjoy will be largely in proportion to the amount of teaching which we receive, and appropriate, at the hands of the Lord.

The untaught Christian is destitute of the deep and unbroken peace which is the inalienable heritage of those who have graduated in Christ's school. As the many objects of fear which, in the mind of the savage, people all lonely places, disappear when he is instructed in truer science: so do doubts and misgivings vanish, as the soul comes to understand its true standing in Jesus.

It is very beautiful to mark the direct teaching agency of the Lord in this passage, and to remember that it is vouchsafed to *all* His children.

There is no teaching to compare with that of a father. The professional schoolmaster is apt to become mechanical. He looks on his pupils as so many brains which he must cram for examination. He finds, therefore, a peculiar charm in the bright and clever ones, who will repay his care; as the virgin soil of the Western States responds luxuriantly to the first scratch of the plough. He is in danger of underrating the value of those who may be dull because they need better food—or because they have come of a race of dullards, stupified by generations of lethargy. The little tired maiden, worn out by nursing the new-born infant; the dull and stupid child; the boy who cannot fix his thoughts; the under-fed and the ill-clad offspring of poverty—these are often scantily attended to. But there is no such partiality with a father; and it has no lodgement in the heart of God. *All* His children are taught. He takes equal care over each. He perhaps takes most care over the stupid ones; putting the lesson in successive modifications, that it may be brought down to their capacity. It is His chosen business to make you know His will; and if He cannot do it in one way, He will in another. "Line upon line; precept upon precept; here a little, there a little."

We are oftenest taught by chastening. As the Psalmist fitly says: "Blessed is the man whom Thou chastenest, O Lord, and teachest him out of Thy law." (Psalm xciv. 12.) It may be, that there would be less need for this chastening, if only we would learn the same lessons in the easier forms in which they are first presented to us. It·is when all other means fail that chastening is employed. But surely it is also true that there are some lessons which can only be learnt in the Garden, and beneath the Shadow of the Cross. The most deeply taught Christians are generally those who have been brought into the searching fires of deep soul-anguish. If you have been praying to know more of Christ, do not be surprised if He takes you aside into a desert place, or leads you into a furnace of pain. God's private mark is always burnt into the spirit in a furnace.

But after all, there is no text more clear or helpful in its teaching on this matter than the one referred to at the heading of this chapter: "The anointing which ye have received of Him abideth in you, and ye need not that any man teach you; but as the same anointment teacheth you of all things, and is truth."

Many amongst us are not able to attend any of those Conferences for the promotion of Christian living, which are so characteristic of the present day, and which are helping to prepare the Bride for the coming of her Lord. And there is sometimes a fear entertained by such, that they will fail to acquire some of those blessed truths, which in these days are being so marvelously unfolded to our ken. But let all such hush their fears, and be encouraged by the assurance of this passage, that the loving and obedient soul need not want any other teacher than the dear Lord Himself.

If the education of the inner life be intrusted to Him, He undertakes that nothing shall be lacking which ought to be known; and that no time should be spent on superfluous ˏor needless studies. The believer, who has the private tuition of the Saviour, will not be less proficient than those who have sat in the highest seats in the school of the church. Yes, and when Christ teaches, He needs no fee or reward. He demands only willingness to obey and perform, as each new item of truth is presented. If we will only put into immediate practice the truths He imparts, there is simply no limit to the blessed lore in which He will instruct us. "Who teacheth like Him?"

There are three points to notice in closing.

1. *Christ teaches by the Holy Ghost.*

It is unmistakable that the Spirit is referred to in this passage as "the anointing which we have received." The inspired symbol for the Holy Ghost, throughout the Bible, is OIL. The oil that was poured on Aaron's head, and descended to the skirts of his garments, spake of Him. The Holy Spirit is, so to speak, the medium by which Jesus dwells in the surrendered heart, and operates through it, and in it. Thank God, we *have* received the Spirit from His hands. And when He gives, He never takes back. There can never be any withdrawal of that which has been bestowed. He *abideth* in you. But though the Spirit can never be withdrawn, He may be quenched and grieved to our unutterable loss. Let us yield to Him, that He may put forth in us all His gracious might.

2. *This teaching is inward.* There are doubtless many lessons taught by Providence. But after all, the meaning of outward events is a riddle, until He opens "the dark sayings on the harp." And the teaching is therefore so quiet, so unobtrusive, so hidden that many an earnest seeker may think

that nothing is being taught or acquired, as the months go on. But we cannot gauge the true amount of progress which we are making from year to year. The teaching is so thoroughly a secret matter between God and the Spirit. But when some great crisis supervenes, some trial, some duty; and the spirit puts forth powers of which it had seemed incapable—there is a swift discovery of the results, which had been slowly accruing during long previous hours.

3. *The main end of this teaching is to secure our abiding in Christ.* "Even as it hath taught you, ye shall abide in Him." All Christian progress begins, continues, and has its fruition here. Severed from Jesus, we can do nothing. Abiding in Jesus, we partake of "the root and fatness" of His glorious life. All His fulness slowly enters into us. What wonder then, that the whole bent of the Holy Spirit's teaching is

to insist upon this prime necessity! And we may well study hard to be proficient in this sacred lore, learning how to abide in Christ, because all Heaven is there. It is thus that God is waiting to teach each of us, His little children. "If thou criest after knowledge, and liftest up thy voice for understanding; if thou seekest her as silver, and searchest for her as hid treasures—then shalt thou find the knowledge of God." (Prov. ii. 3-5.)

X.
"Comforteth."
2 Cor. i. 4.

WHAT a word is this! There is music in the very mention of it. And there is not one of us that cannot appreciate its meaning and worth. In the prophecies of Isaiah, God calls on others to comfort His people and speak comfortably to His chosen; but here He is described as being the sole comforter of His saints. It is as if He refused to wait the consummation of all things, before beginning to wipe away all tears from our eyes, and were already prepared to comfort us as a mother comforteth her first-born.

In God there is the mother-nature, as well as the Fatherhood. All love was first in Him, ere it was lit up in human hearts. The fires that burn so brightly on the altars of motherhood the world over, were lit in the first instance from the Heart of God; and He keeps them alight. And therefore the love that is so quick to detect and so swift to hush the wail of the babe; which is so sensitive to discover that something ails the troubled heart; which is so inventive of little methods of solace, now by tender touch, and again by delicate suggestion—this love is in the great heart of God, and awaits our need to enwrap us in the embrace of an infinite sympathy and comfort.

The apostle had known this many a time; and when he tells out his experiences on this matter, we feel we are listening to one who knew whereof he spake. Few have suffered more than he did, from the moment that he gave up all for Christ, to the hour in which he died a martyr for the faith—the break with old friends; the physical sufferings of his lot; the homelessness, and privations, and continual journeyings; the care of all the churches, the opposition of false brethren. Every epistle bears some evidence of the anguish constantly being inflicted on his noble and tender heart. And yet he said, *God comforteth us.* "Who comforteth in all our tribulations, that we may be able to comfort them which are in any trouble, by the comfort wherewith we ourselves are comforted of God." (2 Cor. i. 4.)

There are many ways in which "the God of all comfort" comforts us. Sometimes He shoots a ray of cheer over the darkened life by a verse of Scripture, sent on a card, or written by a friend; sometimes a passage of Scripture rings in our memory like a sweet refrain, rising and falling as a peal of distant bells heard across a wide valley. Sometimes a gift—which shows that some one is thinking tenderly of us—comes into our hands; and we value it not for its intrinsic worth, but because of the love which prompted it, and which is the symptom of a tenderer love behind. Sometimes an unexpected friend comes into our home, with a bright face and a warm grasp of the hand; and we are comforted of God by the coming of a Titus. (2 Cor. vii. 5, 6.) There is no day so dark, no lot so sad, but that unto it God contrives to put a little scrap of comfort; not enough perhaps to take away the pain, which we need as discipline; but just enough to carry us through the sad hours which move so heavily.

Let us look out for God's rays of comfort. There is never sorrow without its attendant comfort. Only we are often so deeply exercised and engrossed with the sorrow, that we miss the solace. We are so downcast, that we do not see the angel-form waiting by our side. We are too monopolized by grief to be aware of aught beside; and so the light fades from the landscape unobserved, and the sweet singer, who had come to cheer us, steals unnoticed out of our homestead for want of a word of recognition, and a look of grateful acknowledgment.

It is sometimes a mystery why we should be troubled as we are. Why is every chord of sorrow struck within us? Why do we suffer on so many sides of our nature? Why are we touched in the property, which melts before our gaze; and in the home, which becomes darkened by death; and in the person, the body suffering, the heart lacerated and torn? Some go through life without all this. But they are not the noblest characters. No great picture has ever been produced without shadows lurking somewhere on the canvas. No master composer in music or poetry can touch the heart of humanity without having suffered first. But there is a yet deeper reason: some of us are permitted to pass through all kinds of tribulation, that God may have a chance of comforting us; and that we may learn the divine art of comfort, so as to "be able to comfort them which are in any trouble, by the comfort wherewith we ourselves have been comforted of God."

Shall not this thought comfort us when we next pass through any sorrow? The one thing in sorrow which makes it sometimes almost unbearable is its apparent aimlessness. Why am I made to suffer thus? What have I done? Hush, impatient spirit! thou art in God's school of sorrow for a special purpose. Be careful to notice how He comforts thee. Watch His methods. See how He wraps up the broken spirit, with touch so tender, and bandage so accurately adjusted. Remember each text which He suggests—put them down so as not to be forgotten: there will come a time in your life when you will be called on to comfort another afflicted just as you are. Your special sorrow is sent because that which you will be called on to solace, will be of quite an unique and uncommon kind; and your comfort will be required. Without this special discipline yourself, you would be totally non-plussed at the difficulty of your task; but you will have no difficulty henceforth. When the agonized heart comes to you and lays bare its grief, bitterly thinking that it is alone and incomprehensible in its anguish, it will be comforted by hearing that *you* have traversed the over-shadowed pathway, down the deep glen; and you will be able to tell out, step by step, the way in which God comforted you.

O Christian workers, who long to

become adepts in the art of ministering to souls diseased!—be not astonished if your education be long and costly. And since there is no one else to practice on, be prepared to find that God is teaching you how to comfort, by first giving you the pain, and then the comfort which is fitted to allay it. No tongue can tell the tenderness of God. Only let us go to Him more freely; opening up the agony of our hearts. The very telling will relieve us.

But in addition to this, we shall be sensible of delicate alleviations and palliatives, suggested by the ingenuity of a Divine tenderness, which will enable us to endure. And God is never wearied by our querulousness or protracted sufferings. He lingers beside us through the years. He fainteth not, neither is weary. And this shall be true of every hour, however dark—and of every path, however rugged—

"HE COMFORTETH US."

XI.
The Four=Fold Cluster.

JOHN x. 3. 4.

THE figure is borrowed from a fold in some mountain valley, where the flock has rested through the hours of darkness, protected from robbers by the deputy-shepherd (*the porter*), and from the wolves by the barriers of the enclosure.

At last the morning arrives, and with it the shepherd. He comes to the portal. The porter knows his step, and voice, and knock; and opens to him without a moment's hesitation.

The very sheep, more docile and sagacious than those of our northern climes, gave evident signs that they, too, know that their own true shep-

"He calleth and Leadeth."

herd has come, for "they hear his voice."

The shepherd then proceeds to call them out by name. For each has some special name, often suggested by a deformity or a peculiarity in its appearance. And as he mentions it, the bearer, proud to be noticed, comes from among the eager pressing crowd, and passes out from the fold to where the shepherd awaits it, beyond its containing walls. "He calleth his own sheep by name, and leadeth them out."

Thus at last the whole flock emerge from the fold and stand there, in the wild mountain-pass; while the giant forms of the hills, hushed with unbroken silence, covered by bracken and gorse, and haunted by wild game, rise around.

When the shepherd thus put forth his own sheep, "he goeth before them, and the sheep follow him; for they know his voice, And a stranger will they not follow, but will flee from him; for they know not the voice of strangers." It is said that cases of dispute about the ownership of sheep are still settled in the East by putting the flock in the midst of a large field, and by letting the rival claimants call to them from opposite sides, it being a well-known fact that a sheep will always run to that side of the field on which the true shepherd stands.

In all this there is an exquisite parable of the dealings of the Saviour with us.

Who is there that does not know something of the shelter and comfort of the Fold? That home, with all its calm and happy associations; that situation, held so long that its duties have become a sort of second nature; that competence, hardly earned, and large enough to promise years of ease—these are instances of sheltering folds

"His Own Sheep."

in which we rest. But we may not rest in them forever. The grass about a fold is eaten down, and worn with incessant treading; and it is therefore very different to that which, bathed in dew, carpets the mountain sides And so the true Shepherd comes at length, to bring us out of the fold to where the fresh, bright, mountain breezes breathe freely, and life is luxury in the exhilarating air. It is a matter of daily experience. Changes are permitted to pass and repass over our lives, which break up our homes, scatter our nests, shatter our schemes, and drive us forth to the untried and novel experiences which we dread. But in all these changes there is always the personal presence and superintendence of the Good Shepherd, who neither slumbers nor sleeps.

"He calleth His own sheep by name." It is a searching inquiry for us each —Am I one of His own sheep? For

if that is settled in the positive, it involves an untold wealth and weight of blessing. Given to Him, in the eternal ages, by the Father; rescued from the wolf at the cost of the Shepherd's life; endowed with eternal life, so that they can never perish; safe within the hollow of the guarding hand of Jesus, from which neither man, nor devil, can pluck them forth; known intimately and familiarly by Him who loves unutterably; led in to rest, as well as out to work—no mortal tongue can tell or human mind imagine all that Jesus is or does for those whom He designates as *His own sheep*. But this is clear and unmistakable, that the Good Shepherd has an intimate and individual knowledge of us each. He knows us *by our name*.

In the wilderness wanderings, the Almighty God uttered words to Moses which have ever seemed to me to involve a weight of meaning far greater than appears upon their surface. "And the Lord said to Moses, I will do this thing also that thou hast spoken: for thou hast found grace in My sight, *and I know thee by name.*" There is a depth of significance in those words which cannot be expressed, and can only be realized by the glad soul to whom they are spoken. What intimacy! what familiarity! what dignity and glory! None but a friend could call his friend by name! And what must it not be, to be the friend of the Deity itself! Yet all this is sure for any one of us, whom Jesus knows and calls by name.

The prophet compares the starry hosts to a flock of sheep, scattered through the fields of space. "Lift up your eyes on high, and behold who hath created these, that bringeth out their host by number: He calleth them all by names, by the greatness of His might, for that He is strong of power; not one faileth." But surely one, for whom Christ died, is worth more to Him than all the hosts of heaven! And if the stars are so safe, because He is responsible to maintain and guide them, shall not we too be equally safe, whom He calleth *by name?* Would He have entered into such intimate relationship with us, if that were not to issue in an eternal union?

There is one sure sign of the true sheep: "*they know His voice.*" They can distinguish its sweet tones among all other sounds; and to hear is to obey, "*He leadeth them out.*" In heaven He is said to feed the redeemed as a flock, and to *lead* them to living fountains of water; *i. e.*, from one fountain to another, deeper and deeper into the heart of Heaven. But this gracious ministry is equally His work on earth. He is always leading us out—out from the old into the new; out from the familiar to the untried; out from the attained to the unattained; out from experiences and confessions, which have become familiar, to the glorious possibilities of Christian living. These leadings come in many delicate and tender ways — by circumstances, by friendships, by books, by passages of Scripture; but when they come, it will well repay us to obey and follow. There is no experience in the Blessed Life into which Jesus will not lead us, if only we are faithful to the slightest intimation of His will.

"*He putteth forth His own sheep.*" Ah, this is bitter work for Him and us—bitter for us to go; but equally bitter for Him, to cause us pain. Yet it must be done. It would not be conducive to our true welfare to stay always in one happy and comfortable lot. He therefore puts us forth. The nest is broken up, that the young fledglings may be compelled to try their wings and learn to fly. The fold is deserted, that the sheep may wander over the bracing mountain slope. The labourers must be thrust out into the harvest; else the golden grain would spoil. Take heart!—it could not be better to stay, when He determines it otherwise. And if the loving hand of our Lord puts us forth, it must be well. On, in His name, to green pastures, and still waters, and mountain heights!

"*He goeth before them.* Whatever awaits us is encountered first by Him —each difficulty and complication; each wild beast or wilder robber; each yawning chasm or precipitous path. Faith's eye can always discern His majestic presence in front; and when that cannot be seen, it is dangerous to move forward. Bind this comfort to your heart: that the Saviour has tried for Himself all the experiences through which He asks you to pass; and He would not ask you to pass through them unless He was sure that they were not too difficult for your feet, or too trying for your strength. The Breaker always goes up before us. The Woodsman hews a path for us through the trackless forest. The broad-shouldered Brother pushes a way for us through the crowd. And we have only to follow.

This is the Blessed Life—not anxious to see far in front; not careful about the next step; not eager to choose the path; not weighted with the heavy responsibilities of the future: but quietly following behind the Shepherd, *one step at a time.*

XII.
"Our God is a Consuming Fire."
HEBREWS xii. 29.

WHAT comfort there is in these words! Once they only filled us with alarm: now they are the tidings of great joy.

It made a great difference, on the shores of the Red Sea, on which side of the cloud the hosts were placed. To be on the one side meant terror and dismay: "The Lord looked unto the host of the Egyptians through the pillar of fire and of the cloud, and troubled the host of the Egyptians." But to be on the other side mean comfort and hope: "It was a cloud and darkness to them; but it gave light by night to these." Similarly, a great difference is made by our position towards God, as to whether the words at the head of this chapter will be a comfort or a cause of anxiety. If we are against God—enemies in our mind, by wicked works sinning against His gentle, Holy Spirit—we can look for little relief in considering the majestic symbolism of the passage. But if we are on His side, sheltered under His hand, hidden in the cleft of the Rock, conscious that we are in Him that is true—then we may rejoice with exceeding great joy that "our God is a Consuming Fire."

In Scripture FIRE is the invariable symbol of God's nature and character. It was as a lamp of FIRE that the Almighty passed between the pieces of Abraham's sacrifice. It was as FIRE, which needed not the wood of the acacia-bush for its maintenance, that He appeared to Moses in the wilderness, to commission him for his life-work. It was as FIRE that His presence shone on Mount Sinai, in the giving of the law. The Divine acceptance of the sacrifices throughout the ancient ritual was betokened by the FIRE that fell from heaven, and fed upon the flesh of slain beasts. Malachi said that Christ would come as a refiner's FIRE; and when the forerunner announced His advent, he compared it to the work of the ruddy flame, which destroys and purifies: "He shall baptize you with the Holy Ghost and with FIRE." "He will burn up the chaff with unquenchable FIRE." It was, therefore, also in perfect harmony with the entire range of scriptural symbolism, that the Pentecostal descent of the Holy Ghost was accompanied by cloven tongues, like as of FIRE.

Of course, we must not, and would not, deny that there is a punitive and terrible side to all this. It is no light matter to persist in sin. "In flaming fire." He will take "vengeance on them . . . that obey not the Gospel of our Lord Jesus Christ." 'He is terrible in His doing toward the children of men." Fire—which is our most useful ally; which labours for us day and night in our furnaces and fire-places—is harmless and helpful, so long as we obey its laws and observe its conditions: but when once we disobey those laws, and contravene those conditions that which blessed begins to curse, and leaps forth upon us, carrying devastation to all our works, so that the smiling fields become a blackened waste, and our palaces a heap of ruins. So it is with the nature of God. He is gentle, loving, and forbearing: but if a sinner persists in sin, shutting his eyes to the light, and closing his heart to the love of God, then he must needs discover that "with the froward He will show Himself forward." "Kiss the Son, lest He be angry, and ye perish from the way when His wrath is kindled but a little."

But let us turn now to some of those gracious thoughts, which are enshrined in this passage:

Fire searches. Surely this is one of our greatest needs. There is so much of selfishness and sin in the very best of us. Sometimes we get a glimpse of what we are, and turn our thought swiftly away from the horrid spectacle. And what we ourselves dare not contemplate, we carefully hide from the gaze of our tenderest friends. Ah, what pride, what vanity, what self-conceit, are ours!—fretful, if not sufficiently admired; jealous, if outshone; mean enough to take advantage of another, if only we can do it without being found out; capable of the same vile sins which flame out as beacon-lights in those who are not restrained by the same outward bonds as we are.

No malicious critic with biting

words has ever touched the inveterate evil of our hearts, or said a tithe of the truth of us. We have never ourselves realized how bad we are. We need not be surprised at any further discoveries that may rise up to confront us with shame and agony. But it is well to be searched. The ancient motto bade men *know themselves.* The discovery of what we are will drive us most quickly to God for His cleansing and grace. We need not wish to dwell upon our sins, as though health could come by considering disease; but we may gladly accept the searching of the fire of God. Let us know the evil things that are within us. Let us be taught how much wood, hay, and stubble been have built on that foundation, which has undoubtedly been laid in our hearts. Let us submit to the discoveries of disease, which the stethoscope, the searching finger, the probing-knife, will disclose.

O God, who art as fire, search me and know my heart; try me and know my thoughts!

Fire cleanses. Yonder metal is mingled with many inferior ingredients: the earth, in which it has lain for centuries, clings to it; dross depreciates its value. But plunge it into the glowing furnace; raise the heat until the gleaming light is almost intolerable to the gaze; keep it in that baptism of flame—ere long the metal will be cleansed of its impurities, freed from alloy, and fitted for any mould into which you may desire to pour it. Is it not thus that God will deal with us? He is a consuming fire.

In the olden vision, when Isaiah lamented his uncleanness, there flew unto him one of the seraphim, who had taken a live coal from off the altar, which he laid upon his lips, saying, "Lo! this hath touched thy lips;

Fire Transforms.

and thine iniquity is taken away, and thy sin purged." And will not God do as much for us again? We have been cleansed from the stains of our many transgressions: but do we not need this deep, this thorough, this fiery purification?

There are three agents in purification—the Word of God; the Blood of the Son of God; and the Fire of God, which is the Holy Ghost. We know something of the two former: do we know the meaning of the latter? We have been purified by the Water and the Blood: have we passed also through the Fire? "He shall baptize you with the Holy Ghost, and *with Fire*." We cannot define, in so many words, the manner of this sacred operation—it is a matter for holy consciousness: but the heart knows when it has experienced it. It is not that temptation ceases to assail; or that there is no possibility of again yielding to sin; or that the evil tendencies of the old nature are eradicated: but that there is a burning up and consumption of evil things which had been too long permitted to hold sway, and to mar the glory of the work of God in the heart. There is deliverance, where there was bondage; there is purity, where there was corruption; there is love, where there was malice, envy, ill-will.

This blessed operation of the Holy Ghost may be experienced by those who will take no denial, and who by faith claim all that He waits to do for them. Let us, then, appropriate that expressive prayer of Wesley's hymn:

"Refining Fire, go through my heart!"

Fire transforms. That poker lying in your fender is hard, and cold, and black; but if you place it for a few moments in the heart of the fire, it becomes soft, intensely hot, and glowing with the whiteness of incandescence. Take it out again, and all its old qualities will re-assert themselves; but whilst in the fire, they cannot be manifested: the iron is transformed into the likeness of the flame in which it is bathed.

Thus is it with ourselves. By nature we too are hard, and cold, and black; and the tendency of our nature will always be in these directions; waiting to re-assert itself, when left to its own devices.

But if only we can for ever dwell with the devouring fire, and dwell with the everlasting burnings of the Love and Light and Life of God —a wonderful change will pass over us; and we shall be changed into the same image, from glory to glory. No longer hard, we shall be moulded into any shape He selects. No longer cold, we shall glow with love to God and man. No longer black, we shall be arrayed in the whiteness of a purity, which is that of intensest heat.

Too long have we shrunk from the burning, fiery furnace, which is not sorrow, or trial, or pain—but God. Let us get into God. Let us open our nature, that God, the Holy Ghost, may fill us: then shall we become like Himself; our grosser natures shall seem to ascend to heaven in horses and chariots of flame. In God's Fire we shall become Fire.

XIII.
The Spirit's help.
ROMANS viii. 26.

IN that sublime chapter, which touches the whole gamut of the Blessed Life, from the first *No Condemnation* to the final *No Separation*, we have a cluster of Present Tenses, which tell of the incessant working of the Holy Ghost. And we need to ponder them well; because the crying need of the present day among Christians, is a clearer apprehension of the gracious ministry of the Third Person in the ever-blessed Trinity.

The spirit leads us (verse 14).

This is a very dark and difficult world, in which we might soon lose our way, if we were left to ourselves without some inner voice to prompt us and direct our steps. And it would hardly be like our Heavenly Father to leave us to grope our way in the dark. Is it not just what we should have expected, to find that the need is met by the inner promptings of the Holy Ghost? "Led by the Spirit of God" (verse 14). Those leadings may be given in the concurrence of events, in the call of circumstances, or in the application of some verse of Scripture to our hearts; but oftener still, perhaps, in that inner light, and that still, small voice, of which the secret heart is alone aware.

These leadings are never withheld from any perplexed child of God who really needs them, and awaits them in unwavering expectancy. At first they may not be very distinct: but they will glimmer out into light. It is well to wait till they become perfectly clear. "The vision will come; it will not tarry." The only condition to be fulfilled by us is to divest our hearts of all prejudice and self-will; to wean ourselves from natural impulses, as little children; to hold ourselves open to take any course which He may suggest: and we shall know, by glad and certain experience, the leadings of the Holy Spirit.

The Spirit bears witness that we are children of God (verse 16).

The method of this witness has been often misunderstood. Men have listened for some mystic voice, which should speak within their heart, saying, "Thou art a child." And because they have listened for it in vain, they have been ready to despair. But this blessed witness is rather an *impression* than a voice; a *conviction* wrought into the fabric or texture of the spirit; an *assurance* which, as the years go by, testing it, becomes a bulwark on which the waves of doubt break harmlessly into clouds of spray.

And the subject-matter of which the Spirit witnesseth is not, primarily, that we are children, but that God is our Father. He teaches us to call God "Father." He moulds our lips into the child-like cry, *Abba*. He compels us to launch away from the thought of our childship on to the ocean of His Fatherhood. Beneath His searching, God in Christ becomes infinitely lovable and delightful; perfect love casteth out fear; the heart turns to Jehovah with the freedom of a child to a father, and thus insensibly our attitude towards God becomes the best evidence that we are His children.

The Spirit helpeth our infirmities (verse 26).

Never do we feel them more than at the hour of prayer. Sometimes our thoughts scatter like a flock of sheep;

The Spirit's Help.

or flag and faint before the spiritual effort of stirring ourselves up to take hold on God. Who does not have times, when (to use Jeremy Taylor's similitude) prayer is like the rising of a lark against an east wind? We even tire in maintaining the attitude of devotion: and how much more its spirit! We know not what to pray for; we are ignorant of the best arguments to employ; we ask amiss; we cannot keep in the perpetual spirit and temper of devotion; we lack that calm faith, which can leave its burden at the mercy-seat, and be at rest.

In all this the Spirit helpeth us. He "helpeth our infirmities." Knowing the mind of God, He is aware of those things which it will please our Father to bestow, and which indeed are only waiting for us to ask them at His hand. These He suggests to us; for these He excites strong and passionate desire; with respect to these

He leads us to pour out our souls in importunate and prevailing prayer.

When next you are sensible of a mighty tide of desire rising up in your heart, bearing you forward on its bosom toward God, yield to it; let it have its blessed way with you. Though there be almost pain in the unutterable passion of desire, dare not to restrain it; for the Holy Spirit is then taking you up into the purposes of God, and is leading you to ask those things which lie near His heart, and which brood over you as clouds of blessing ready to break. This is true prayer: the attempt on the part of man to tell out the deep, unutterable thoughts, which the Spirit is inspiring within.

The Spirit maketh intercession with groanings that cannot be uttered (verse 26).

Goethe said, that when he stood alone amid the scenes of nature, she seemed to be like an imprisoned captive sighing to be redeemed. Some such thought seemed present to the Apostle, when he spoke of the groaning of creation, and the groaning of the saints.

But how passing wonderful to be told of the groaning of the Spirit!—not the groans of death; but the travail groans of birth, ushering in a new creation. Ah! no one can estimate the pain which our sins and sorrows cost God. "It grieved Him to His heart." "I know their sorrows." "In all their affliction, He was afflicted." And out of all this spring the intercessions which the Spirit maketh in and for the saints; and which sometimes almost break down the human spirit in which they strive for utterance. What do we not owe to those mighty and unutterable pleadings? How many a time have they brought untold blessings into our hearts and lives! We did not realize their source: but had we realized it, we would have prized more gratefully those gentle yet mighty operations.

All the mightiest and saintliest of God's children have been most aware of the infinite distance between their noblest attainments in experience of prayer, and the ultimate splendour and fulness of God. The biography of one of the best is entitled "Confessions."* He knows little of the Christian life, who is always conscious of being able to express all he feels. The joy is sometimes unspeakable; the peace passeth all understanding.

But all these are signs of the presence of the Holy Spirit in the heart. And all He is doing there, unutterable and glorious as it is, is the outcome of the will of God, and therefore certain to be realized some day in fact.

"HE MAKETH INTERCESSION FOR THE SAINTS ACCORDING TO THE WILL OF GOD."

*Augustine.

XIV.
𝔗𝔥𝔢 𝔖𝔭𝔦𝔯𝔦𝔱 𝔏𝔲𝔰𝔱𝔢𝔱𝔥 𝔞𝔤𝔞𝔦𝔫𝔰𝔱 𝔱𝔥𝔢 𝔉𝔩𝔢𝔰𝔥."

GALATIANS V. 17.

WE are not in the flesh; but the flesh is in us. This seems to be the incontrovertible testimony of Scripture and experience.

Writing to the Galatian Christians, the Apostle makes use of an expression which shows that, in his estimation, taught by the Holy Ghost, there was no eradication of the principle of the old nature, known as *the flesh*. He says: "The flesh lusteth against the spirit." Evidently, therefore, it was a matter of continual experience, with Him and them: he speaks of it as a matter concerning which there can be no dispute.

Those who teach the eradication of the self-life, often beg the question by asking if God, who has done so much, could not also root out the old fleshly principle of the self-life. To this question there is but one answer: of course He could. But to ask the question is to raise a false issue. It is not what God can do, but what He chooses to do. And so far as I can understand the Bible, it does not teach that the eradication of the flesh is God's intention for us on this side of the gates of pearl.

But *this* is God's intention, as clearly taught in Romans vi.—we who believe are accounted as one with Jesus:

> "One when He died; one when He rose;
> One when He triumphed o'er His foes;
> One when in heaven He took His seat,
> And Heaven rejoiced o'er Hell's defeat."

Therefore, having died in Him, we

have, by death, passed out of the realm of sin. "He that is dead is freed from sin." In God's thought and intention, we are where Christ is, on the other side of death; and therefore for ever delivered from the bondage and claims of sin. And now it is our duty by faith to make God's thought ours. We must reckon ourselves to be dead indeed unto sin, and alive unto God. It is not that the sin-principle (the old man) is dead in us; but we must be dead to it. Whenever it arises, we are to account ourselves as being insensible to its claims: as a corpse is to the tears of warm affection, or to the winsome embraces of a love that cannot part.

Does not this command, *Reckon yourselves dead*, prove that the old man has not ceased to exist? If it had, then it would have been needless to *reckon* ourselves dead to it. The necessity of *reckoning* ourselves dead proves that it is still present within us, requiring from us an attitude of constant denial and abhorrence and disregard.

But how can we take up and maintain this attitude? It is an impossibility to those who have not learnt to live in the power of the Holy Ghost.

Listen to these striking testimonies of Scripture:

"The law of THE SPIRIT OF LIFE in Christ Jesus hath made me free from the law of sin and death." (Rom. viii. 2.)

"If ye THROUGH THE SPIRIT do mortify the deeds of the body, ye shall live." (Rom. viii. 13.)

"Walk IN THE SPIRIT, and ye shall not fulfil the lust of the flesh." (Gal. v. 16.)

We have also the assurance of the succeeding verse, that if the flesh lusteth against the Spirit, the Spirit lusts back again, and more mightily, against the flesh, so that we may not do the things which otherwise we should. (See Gal. v. 17, R. V.) How gladly may we dwell upon this glorious present tense! Where the Christian is living in the fullness of the Spirit, the flesh has no chance. It is within him; it may strive to entice him (James i. 14); it may even stretch out its hands in answer to the solicitation of the devil from without; but it is carefully watched by the Holy Ghost. Its every movement is resisted. It is kept down by His gracious energy. It is quelled so instantly that the spirit is hardly conscious of its strivings. And the power of the flesh, as the years go past, becomes so broken, that it is but the attenuated skeleton of its former self. Thus we are kept from doing what otherwise, and if left to ourselves, we should be certain to do. Nothing but the divine power of the Holy Ghost could keep us from being swept away before the lustings of the flesh.

Some years ago, I lived in a house, the underground kitchen of which was so damp that, when we failed to keep up a vigorous fire, the floor was encrusted with white mould, so much so that the maid could fill her dust-pan with it; but when the fire was burning bright and warm, the bricks and walls were kept perfectly dry. There was always the latent tendency to produce damp; but it was kept in abeyance by the heat, so it could not do as it otherwise would. So when the Holy Ghost, as fire, works mightily within the heart, those tendencies to sin, which are, alas! natural to us, are overcome and thwarted, and kept in the place of death.

In an infected house, the carbolic acid plentifully distributed in basins and on sheets acts as an antiseptic to the germs coming from the patient's body, so that they are prevented doing what otherwise they would to healthy subjects. The blessed Spirit is the antiseptic to the evil of the old nature.

The Holy Ghost is in every Christian. "If any man have not the Spirit of Christ, he is none of His." But in many He is cribbed into a narrow space; confined in an attic or a cellar of their souls; and therefore He cannot do for them what He would. If that has been so, and if, therefore, your life has been one of failure and disappointment, open every department and room of your being to His gracious operations.

And as mercury, when poured into a glass of water, will expel the water and take its place, so will the Holy Spirit take possession of your being, filling you, as on the day of Pentecost He filled the waiting disciples: and then He will dwell within you mightily; keeping pure and holy the body, which is His peculiar Temple.

XV.
Upbraideth Not.
JAMES I. 5.

IS not that like God? It is much for Him to give; more for Him to give liberally; most for Him not to upbraid the suppliants—because it is just here that so many well-meaning men brush off the exquisite bloom from the luscious fruits of their gifts.

We upbraid. We upbraid men that they are not more provident; that they come so often; that they ask so much. We make our aid the occasion for a reprimand or a lecture. We keep suppliants waiting until we have administered the reproof which we imagine their case demands; or have reminded them of the many instances of past

The Prodigal.

ingratitude and sin. But there is nothing like that in God.

We may go to Him a thousand times in a single day; but He will never upbraid us with coming too often. We may go to Him with needs immense as the ocean's bed; but He will never upbraid us with asking too much. We may go to Him after years of ingratitude and neglect; but He will never upbraid us with the past. It will never be so much as mentioned by Him; though His loving-kindness will bring it more to our minds than His severest censures.

What a blessing it was for the prodigal that he did not meet his elder brother before his father! Had the two, by any sad mischance, met face to face in the field, it is certain that the ragged wanderer would never have gone another step. His brother would have upbraided him with leaving home, and wasting his patrimony, and coming back in so disgraceful a state. Assuredly he would not have killed the fatted calf; but he would have killed all hope in that sad and sin-stained soul. With one farewell glance at the dear old home, the penitent would have turned back to the far-country and the swine. Those upbraidings would have broken the bruised reed, and quenched the smoking flax in densest midnight.

But mercifully the prodigal first met his father, whose heart had never ceased to yearn for him, and whose eye strove against the blinding touch of grief and years, that it might still scan the road along which that prodigal child had gone. Was there upbraiding in his look or tone? Never! Was there upbraiding mingled with the first glad notes of welcome? Not a trace! Not a word about the long absence, the unbroken silence, the wasted wealth, the wild and evil life!

If the son had had his way, he would have carried his confession to the end, and chosen for himself the servant's lot; but even in that he was stopped, and silenced with the warm rush of his father's love. "He gave liberally, and upbraided not."

This is a true picture of God. He gives, and gives again. He gives tears and blood. He gives His darling and His All. And yet when men ask more, and demand from Him years of forbearance and patience, He still gives without flinching or chiding; in the firm desire to give the sinner no loop-hole for excuse, no ground for persistence in sin.

Tender love has sometimes changed to gall; and turning on the one to whom once it clung, but who has abused its trust, has bitterly upbraided the neglect, the abuse, the cruelty of years, in words which sting like fire. But the love of God beareth all things, believeth all things, hopeth all things, endureth all things—and "upbraideth not." Do not stay away, then, because your heart condemns you, or because you have abused His gifts in the past: the only upbraidings you need fear are those that may be uttered by your own heart for not having come before.

These words ("upbraideth not") were principally spoken in reference to our need of wisdom—an incessantly recurring need! We are as little children groping in the dark. We have never before been along this road. We are daily being tested by difficulties we cannot master, and problems we cannot solve. How can we thread our way through a maze so intricate as this wondrous human life? Where is the man who is so reliant on his own sagacity as to be perfectly able to trust his own decisions? Do we not need some wise and ever-accessible Mentor and Friend, who shall teach us just how to act when the road forks, and the sign-posts are wanting?

What a comfort, then, it is to know that whenever we lack wisdom we may come to God for it! We may have come very often before; but we may come again. We may need a great deal of patient teaching; but we need not be abashed. We may be very stupid, and require to have things put very simply and clearly, as to an idiot child; but God will never count the trouble one whit too much. We may not have previously acted on the advice given us; but we may come again, as though for the first time, sure of a hearty welcome, a sympathetic hearing, a liberal supply of wisdom. "He upbraideth not."

The wisdom may not be given in advance, or in the form we might have thought; but it will be given just when the answer must be returned, or the step taken. It shall be given in the strong impression on the heart; in the clear conviction of duty; in the concurrence of circumstances; in the indication of slight symptoms which could only be discerned by the eye fixed steadfastly on the eye of God. "It shall be given.' None will be able to gainsay, or refute, or resist the wisdom thus bestowed. It will be like that gift whose presence in Solomon instantly betrayed itself to the world. "They saw that the wisdom of God was in him."

And the time will never come, when in this or any other respect, there shall be any lack to those who seek the Lord; for

'HE GIVETH TO ALL LIBERALLY,
AND UPBRAIDETH NOT."

XVI.
"All Things Are Yours."
1 Corinthians iii. 21.

ALL things serve the man that serves Jesus Christ, the great Servant of God. That seems to be something like the meaning of the words with which St. Paul closes his argument here. We may not follow now the successive steps of that argument, which has been forged in his glowing heart; but we may appropriate this sublime conclusion: "All are yours; and ye are Christ's; and Christ is God's."

The primary thought is not possession or proprietorship; for though that is true of the relation between us and Christ, it is not true of the relation between Christ and the Father.

And evidently these clause-links are constructed upon the same model, because those whom they connect stand in the same relation to one another. What then, is that common relation which binds all things to us, in the same way as we are bound to Christ, and Christ to God the Father?

There is but one common ground on which these clauses stand; and that is *Ministry*, or service—the golden thread that runs through all creation, making it one. The ancient fable told that all things were bound by golden chains about the feet of God: and surely the real, deep connection of which the fable spoke is to be found in the service which each lower order of creation renders to the one above— the service becoming rarer and more refined as the pyramid of existence tapers to a point.

As the Son of Man, *our Lord was also the Servant of God.* "Behold My

Servant whom I uphold." "The God of our fathers hath glorified His Servant Jesus." (Acts iii. 13, R. V.) And His august service is surely sketched in words which foretell that He will put down all rule and authority, and power, and deliver up the Kingdom to God, even the Father. He was amongst men "as one that serveth." But His service is continued still. He girds Himself with a towel to wash our feet; He breaks again the bread of His own life, and puts to our lips the chalice of His own blood, He busies Himself in our cares, and wants, and work. And in ministering to us, He is surely fulfilling also the will of the Father, with whom He is one—God as well as man, in the ever-blessed Trinity. In such senses the life of our blessed Lord is even now one of incessant ministry.

In this same sense, we are His servants. "Ye are Christ's." We are, of course, His, in the sense of being owned by Him: He made us; He bought us; He claims us. But how many of us resemble Onesimus, the runaway slave of Philemon!—who probably bore the brand of his master, and had certainly been purchased by his gold; but who withheld from him his service, following the bent of his own wayward will, and herding with the most abandoned of the populace, that rotted in the criminal quarters of ancient Rome. We too have been bought by the Lord, at priceless cost; but we are far from serving Him with the same sort of loyal and whole-hearted ministry with which He, in His unwearied solicitude for us, serves God.

We know little of those high themes which now engross Him; but we can understand a little better the aims and character of His early life. Let us take these as our model, day by day. He had no plan or pattern of His own, but was content to work out the will of His Father: let us work out *His* will, hourly suggested to us. He, as it were, suppressed His own glorious Self, that the Father who dwelt in Him might work through Him: let us no longer live, but let Christ live His life in us. He sacrificed all, that He might finish the work of Him who sent Him: let us count nothing too great a sacrifice if only we may hear Him say, "Well done, good and faithful servant!" In these and in many ways we may make His service a model of our own. Nay, better still, we may let Him repeat His life of ministry through us, and fulfil in us His perfect ideal.

But whenever we get into this right attitude towards our Lord Jesus we shall find that all things begin to minister to us in a constant round of holy service. Each event or circumstance in life becomes an angel, laden with blessed helpfulness, bringing to us the gifts of our beloved Master.

That title, "Rabboni, Master," the sweetest name by which the prostrate soul can address its Saviour, does not degrade or demean it; but enables it, like the babe Christ, to be the recipient of costly presents sent from afar—gold and spices, frankincense, and myrrh. If you have been chafing at your lot, thinking that time and things are robbing you, you may be sure that you are not as you should be towards Christ; and the true cure will be to get as a slave to His feet. Then all things will be "yours" in this deep sense.

"*Whether Paul, or Apollos, or Cephas.*" Each of these names stands for a distinct species of teaching— the argumentative, the eloquent, the hortative. Do not pass any of them by; from those with whom you have least sympathy, you may glean something. Each disciple brings some bits of bread and fish. Each stone flashes some colour needed by the prism to effect the beam of perfect light. Each flower may furnish some ingredient for the common store of honey.

"*Or the world.*" This is our school, hung with maps, and diagrams, and simple lessons. There is not a single flower, nor a distant star, nor a murmuring brooklet, nor a sound sweet or shrill; there is not a living creature, or a natural process, that may not serve us; not only by meeting some appetite of sense, but of teaching us such deep lessons as those which Jesus drew from the scenes around Him, saying, "The kingdom of heaven is like.

"*Or life, or death.*' When life is lit up in some new young being, it may seem to involve you in a perpetual service, for which you obtain no adequate return. But this is in the outward seeming only: there is a yet deeper sense in which that tiny babe ministers to you; in suggesting deeper thoughts of life, and its meaning and destiny; in revealing to you something of the tie between God and your own soul, which calls Him Father. And death, though it appear to rob you, really enriches you—by making permanent feelings of resignation, and trust, and anticipation, which are not natural to man.

"*Or things present, or things to come.*" How quickly the incidents of daily life are gliding over us! and as they pass, to our weak gaze they steal from us so much that we hold dear— the elastic step, the clear vision, the strong nerve, the beloved friend, the hard-earned gold.

Sometimes they manifestly enrich us. For the young there is a constant sense of acquisition. One good and perfect gift follows swiftly on the heels of another. But when we have crossed the summit of life's hill there is an incessant consciousness of loss.

Yet, in God's sight, and in the spiritual realm, these distinctions vanish and pass away as mists under the touch of the sun: and we find that all incidents come to bless us; all winds waft us to our haven; all tribes bring their tribute into the throne-room of our inner being.

We are not the creatures of circumstances; but their masters, their kings, their lords. All these things are the servants and tutors appointed by our Father, to wait on and minister to us, His heirs.

"ALL THINGS ARE YOURS."

XVII.
Working Together for Good.
THE KEEN SIGHT OF LOVE.

ROMANS viii. 28.

IT is not given to all men to look behind the phenomena of daily life, and to see into the methods and purposes of God. This is the prerogative of those who love.

Love is quick to catch the meaning of a hint, a gesture, a whisper. Love has an instinctive apprehension of secrets, too deep for words to convey. Love can afford to wait the unfolding of those deepest thoughts, which eye hath not seen, nor ear heard, nor the heart of man conceived. Love is the befitting atmosphere in which the Spirit of Love can brood, who is also

Self-Searching. 147

the spirit of knowledge and revelation, and who teacheth as none other can. If you would know, you must love.

Do you love? Can you answer without a moment's doubt the question—"Lovest thou Me?" The materials for the answer cannot be discovered in emotion or ecstacy, which may some day disappear—as light dying off the hills; or a tropical stream suddenly absorbed into the volcanic hollows beneath its bed. Not there, but here, is there a growing sense of God's personal love to you, and of His parental care? Are you more sensitive to the presence of sin in yourself and others? Do His commandments inspire you with a more quiet and entire obedience? His day—His book—His people—are these more to you than once the scenes of worldly pleasure? If so, you love Him; and that love will grow.

And as it grows in lengthening

years, you will become aware that, after all, it is not yours, but His—the reflection of His love, the beam of His love, which has smitten your heart and been flashed off; as a ray of sunshine will sometimes strike a pane in the window of a distant cottage, and shine there as a point of light, seen from the distance of many miles. It is the outcome of His eternal purpose, which he purposed in Himself in the eternal ages. Oh, marvellous origin of the love of our poor hearts, which has wrought through our calling; and has effected such a result in those who otherwise had been loveless indeed—unloving and unloved!

LOVE DISCERNS THE WORKING OF GOD'S PLAN WHEN ALL SEEMS MOST STILL.

"*We know that things work.*" However stationary the stars appear to be in the blue heavens, we know that they are really sailing onward, with great velocity, in their destined courses. The ocean may seem to sleep at our feet, but in reality it is in a state of incessant activity; its tides and currents perpetually passing to and fro on their appointed ministries. There is not a silent nook within the deepest forest glade, which is not the scene of marvellous activity, though detected only by the educated sense of the naturalist.

So there are times when our lives lack variety and incident. The stream creeps sluggishly through the level plain. Monotony, common-place, dull routine, characterize our daily course. We are disposed to think that we are making no progress; learning no fresh lessons; standing still as the sun over Gibeon; or going back as the shadow on the dial of Ahaz. The child gets impatient, because every day it has to play the same scales.

Then love steps in, and sees that God

is busily at work, maturing His designs, and leading the life forward, though insensibly, into regions of experience, which surpass all thought. The day is breaking; the ice is giving; the picture is advancing; things are moving. God is working all things after the counsel of His own will.

LOVE DISCERNS THE COMPREHENSIVENESS OF GOD'S PLAN.

"*We know that* ALL *things work.*" Men are fond of distinguishing between general and particular providences. They are willing to acknowledge the finger of God in some striking event; or in the swift flashing out of God's sword of justice. They do not hesitate to admit that life as a whole is under God's direction; but they hesitate to say that He is concerned with its ordinary common-places, valueless as the sparrow's fall, slight as the hair of the head. Miles if you like; but not steps.

But love refuses to believe this teaching. It looks on it as practical atheism. It feels that God cannot afford to let the thread of its life pass from His hands for a single moment. The fabric of the character cannot for an instant be taken from God's looms. The moment when God ceased to hold a work would be the moment of irreparable wreckage and harm. Besides, love refuses to believe that its destinies can be absent from the hand and heart of God, though but for the twinkling of an eye; or that a single thing could happen except as He planned, and determined, and permitted. Her quick eye sees Him ever about her path, and her lying down, and acquainted with all her ways.

The spirit thus seems no longer to deal with persons and things; but only with God. It sees no more second causes; because its range of view is filled by the Great First Cause. It finds the will of God, either permitting or enacting, in every event, however trivial, that crosses its path. Everything becomes the vehicle through which God comes near and speaks; everything is intended for some wise and loving purpose; everything is one of the turns of the wheel in the hand of the great Potter, who is fashioning rough clay into a vessel for the royal palace.

LOVE DISCERNS THE HARMONY OF GOD'S PLAN.

"*We know that all things work* TOGETHER." To the eye of sense, things seem contrary the one to the other: the North wind against the South; the frost against the spring's outburst in bud and blossom; tears against smiles. But love detects the harmony of all things; and sees that they work together like the wheels of some huge machinery, which revolve in different directions, cog in cog, but which are hastening forward an identical result.

When the physician has prescribed some medicine, you go to the chemist to have it made up; and he takes one ingredient from this phial, and another from that, and another from elsewhere: any one of these, taken alone, might kill you outright; but when they have been well compounded and mixed, they work together for a perfect cure.

Do not ask in dark suspicion how this one thing can be for your good. Wait to see the other things with which the great Physician is about to balance it. There are wondrous compensations in His dealings with His children. It is not one thing by itself; but one thing put with another thing, and that with a third, and that with a fourth, and all these together, that work your good.

You cannot see the beauty in those sombre tints; but wait till they are relieved by dashes of colour. You shiver before the wintry blast; but that will work with summer zephyrs to produce the autumn fruit. You refuse to be comforted beneath some afflicting blow; but if you can only hush your impatience till you see the blessing with which it is to be combined, you will feel that it was well worth your while to have the bitter, if it were needed, as the basis of a wine of life, so sweet to the taste.

LOVE DISCERNS THE BENEVOLENCE OF GOD'S PLAN.

"*We know that all things work together* FOR GOOD." Disastrous indeed, and adverse, does God's Providence sometimes seem. Stroke on stroke. Blow on blow. Tidings on tidings of dismay. And as the loved ones carry Lazarus to the grave, though they dare not speak out what they think, they cannot help feeling it to be a little hard that they should be allowed to suffer thus, by One who had never been known to tarry, when sickness or death needed His help. Can all this be for good? What good can such things bring?

Then FAITH comes to the aid of LOVE, and reasons of God's Love and Faithfulness. He gave His Son: can He withhold any good thing? He is good: can He give aught but good and perfect gifts? He loves: can He permit any hurt to come to those who are dear to Him as the blood of Calvary? Have not all His dealings in the past been only good? Is not the united testimony of the saints of all ages to the invariable beneficence of His dealings, when they have been allowed to work themselves out to their golden conclusion? Does not the Word of God guarantee the "peaceable fruit of righteousness" to those who submit lovingly to His chastisement?

And thus Love is reassured, and looks away from the discipline to the face of Him that uses the scourge;

and as she watches it closely, she sees beneath the frown, which He wears as a visor, the glances of answering love, the falling of pitying tears. It is hard for Him to maintain the disguise. He could not do as He does unless He loved with a love which is wise, and firm, and strong, just because it is so deep. And thereafter love does not hesitate to pronounce of everything, however dark: "Even so, Father: it seemeth good to Thee, and it is also good to me."

Even in this life we may live to reap the far-off harvest of good, the product of the sowing of tears. But if not, we may surely reckon on doing so in that world where God will unveil to us His plan; and tell us His reasons; and explain to us His hidden meaning; and wipe away all tears from our eyes.

XVIII.

I am the First and the Last.

REVELATION i. 17.

WE have attempted an impossible task in discussing the theme which has stood at the head of this series of articles. And so at last we relinquish our attempt, declaring ourselves defeated—and well we may; because God lives in the Present Tense: He is the I Am: He knows not a Past, and anticipates no Future: He is the same yesterday, to-day, and forever.

All His dealings and promises move on the pivot of the word NOW: and therefore, to discuss the Present Tenses of the Blessed Life—is to attempt to pour the ocean of His infinity into the narrow earthen cup, which we have held to the thirsty lips of His children in these few chapters.

And yet, as we turn away from our unworthy attempt, we cannot forbear saying a few broken words on one of the noblest of them all; and one which seems to comprehend them all, as a ray of sunlight comprehends, interwoven in its texture, the seven-fold beams which make up the prismatic band.

It was the lone isle of Patmos, washed by the Ægean: the light of the sun seemed brighter to the exiled Apostle, because it shone upon the day of resurrection: and as he thought of the loved circle, which was meeting on the other side of the dissevering sea, and longed for the world where the sea should be no more, he was startled by the glory of a light beyond that of the meridian sun: and there stood before him the form of One on whose bosom he had leaned in earlier days, with confiding love; but who was now marvellously and gloriously changed.

That voice, which once faltered in dying agony, had in it a volume of sound like many waters. The face once marred with bitter anguish, shone as the sun. Those feet once nailed to the bitter cross, were bright with the glory of burnished brass. In those hands that once were bound by cruel thongs, glistened the stars of the Churches. Whilst the breast on which St. John had been wont to lean, was girt about with the insignia of the dignity of His office. Was it wonderful that the beloved Apostle fell at His feet as one dead, and needed to be raised by those hands and re-assured by that voice?

What music there was in those words!—"Fear not: I am the First and the Last!" What infinite conceptions cluster around those simple words, far-reaching as eternity, and infinite as God! Jesus Christ is the *sum of all being*; the alphabet of all existence; the Creator and the Final Cause of all creation. "He is before all things;" and "for His pleasure they are and were created." The first germ of being was originated by His creative hand; and when this frame of nature has run its course, and fulfilled its purpose, it is He who will speak the word of dissolution, and bid it cease, and sink back into the nothingness from which it came.

Is He not equally the First and the Last in the *Scheme of Redemption?* When the first thought of it arose in the heart of God (speaking after the manner of men), Christ was there. Every step in the unfolding of the mighty scheme bears the mark of His finger. No other hand has been permitted to intrude into the execution of this masterpiece of Love. He laid the foundations of salvation in the depths of His agony; and every succeeding course in the structure has been laid by Him: and He will bring forward the top-stone, amidst shouting of "Grace, Grace unto it!"

And this is also true in the history of *our personal salvation.* It was He who originated the first desire for better things—as the first ray of light in the chaos of the primeval ages. And it is to His grace that we must attribute every virtue we possess; every holy aspiration; and every blessed lesson in the divine life. Yes, and beneath His hand we are to develop in growing years, till we come to the dividing-line between time and eternity: then He who was the Author of faith in us, will be its Finisher; His face will shine as the bright day-star heralding the eternal morning. And whatever height of blessedness we attain, He will ever be before us, as a something beyond our highest attainment, beckoning us forward: for He must ever be the Last to those for whom He has been the First.

"Fear not!" says this Glorious One. "Fear not! you will need nothing outside of Me. Fear not! I am all-sufficient. Fear not! all others may drop away, leaving you as the sole survivor of your generation: but I will be always the same, and remain with you to the last. Fear not! Time, and Life, and Earth, may pass away; but I will be at the end of all, as I was at the beginning. All things seen may dissolve as the phantasmagoria of cloud and, from which the hues of sunset have faded; but I shall remain, as the Rock of Eternity, which can never move from its solid base, or know the shadow of a change. Fear not! Fear not! Fear not! I will never, never leave thee; I will never, no never, no never, forsake thee!"

Oh, who shall fear, when He stands by, uttering such words as these!

But before we can derive from them their full weight of comfort, we need to make Him the First and the Last of every enterprise; of every act of every day—aye, of every hour. Let everything be begun, continued, and ended, in Him. Let His counsel be sought on the threshold; His succour on the prosecution; and His blessing at the close. Let Him be the star of every morning and of every eve. No man need fear when that is so; for He is impregnable. We may well fear when we step out on a new enterprise, or initiate a new scheme, or begin a new day, without Him; and close without His benediction of peace.

But when He is the Alpha and Omega of all; First, and Last, and Midst; "all and in all"; then heart may fail. and flesh may faint, and difficulties gather; but the spirit may still press on with undaunted courage, whilst He whispers "FEAR NOT!"

Works by Dr. A. J. Gordon.

"Dr. Gordon is a writer with whom to differ is better and more suggestive than to agree with some others. He loves the truth, he gives his readers much that is true and deeply of the essence of Christianity."—THE INDEPENDENT.

The Holy Spirit in Missions. 12mo, cloth, gilt top............................... 1.52

Ecce Venit; Behold He Cometh. 12mo, paper, net 50c.; cloth, gilt top................. 1.25

"It is impossible to read this book without being stimulated by it and getting higher views of some aspects of Christianity."—*The Independent.*

In Christ; or, The Believer's Union with His Lord. *Seventh Edition.* 12mo, paper, net 35c.; cloth, gilt top.......................... 1.00

"We do not remember since Thomas a Kempis a book so thoroughly imbued with a great personal love to Christ."—*The Boston Courier.*

The Ministry of Healing; or, Miracles of Cure in All Ages. *Third Edition.* 12mo, paper, net 50c.; cloth, gilt top................. 1.25

"Dr. Gordon marshals witnesses from all ages in favor of his belief that cures may still be wrought through prayer."—*Evangelical Review.*

The Two-Fold Life; or, Christ's Work for Us, and Christ's Work in Us. 12mo, paper, net 50c.; cloth, gilt top...................... 1.25

"Distinguished by deep spiritual insight, and by great strength of practical argument."—*The Baptist Magazine.*

Grace and Glory. Sermons for the Life That Now Is and That Which Is to Come. 12mo, paper, net 50c.; cloth, gilt top............ 1.50

"Here we have power without sensationalism; calm thought, living and earnest, expressed in forcible language.—*C. H. Spurgeon.*

The First Thing in the World; or, The Primacy of Faith. 16mo, vellum paper covers... .20

Cheaper edition, popular vellum series, net .10

"It is a clear testimony to the vital importance of faith, and we trust it may be read and circulated largely."—*The Episcopal Recorder.*

New York. **FLEMING H. REVELL COMPANY,** Chicago.

"These little books are of priceless value. They are crowded with gems of thought, and breathe a rich spiritual influence."—*Journal and Messenger.*

THE DRUMMOND SERIES OF POPULAR VELLUM BOOKLETS.

Every issue of this popular series is a gem of large worth in choice setting.

Love: The Greatest Thing in the World. By Prof. H. Drummond,
Faith: The First Thing in the World. By A. J. Gordon, D. D.
Hope: The Last Thing in the World. By A. T. Pierson, D. D.
Perfected Life: The Greatest Need of the World. By Prof. H. Drummond.
How to Learn How. By Prof. H. Drummond.
Fight of Faith: Cost of Character. By Theo. Cuyler, D. D.
The Two Men. By Prof. Jas. Stalker.
Temptation. By Prof. Jas. Stalker.
Power from on High. By B. Fay Mills.
How to Become a Christian. By Lyman Abbott, D. D.
The Dew of thy Youth. By J. R. Miller, D.D.
The Last Page of an Officer's Diary.
The Startled Sewing Society. By Mrs. L. H. Crane.
Message of Jesus to Men of Wealth. By Geo. D. Herron, D. D.
Wanted—Antiseptic Christians. A plea for purity of life and walk. By Maud Ballington Booth.

16mo., each 32 pages, vellum paper, edges turned in, each 20c.; with very choice hand-painted floral designs on covers, each, 50c.
*Cheaper paper edition, each, 10c.; per dozen, $1.00.

Fleming H. Revell Company.

Books for Young Men.

Uniform in style and price, 12mo cloth, each 50 cts.

Thoroughness. Talks to Young Men. By Rev. Thain Davidson, D.D.
CONTENTS:—Heartiness, Prosperity and Presumption, Quiet Meditation, Chums, Fools I have Met, Hasting to be Rich, As the Man so is his Strength, The Divine Plumb-line, A Notable Eleven, The Compendium of Christian Duty, Keeping the Heart with Diligence, The Complete Life, The Bow of Promise.

Moral Muscle and How to Use It. A Brotherly Chat with Young Men. By Frederick A. Atkins.
"It looks the facts of young men's lives full in the face, and proclaims the gospel of industry, perseverance, self-control, and manly Christianity."—*St. Andrew's Cross.*

First Battles and How to Fight Them. Some Friendly Chats with Young Men. By Frederick A. Atkins.
"It is true in its substance, attractive in its style, and admirable in its spirit. I heartily commend this little volume."—REV. JOHN HALL, D.D.

Brave and True. Talks to Young Men. By Rev. Thain Davidson, D.D.
"A short series of plain, wholesome, spiritually and temporally elevating talks to young men."—*The Congregationalist.*

The Spiritual Athlete and How He Trains. By W. A. Bodell. Introduction by Rev. B. Fay Mills.
"Its power and value lie in the consistent carrying out of the comparison between physical and spiritual training."—*The Independent.*

Turn Over a New Leaf, and Other Words to Young People at School. By B. B. Comegys.
"The Author makes the subject fascinating and there are thousands just now who should turn over the leaf."—*The Western Christian Advocate.*

Fleming H. Revell Company.

WORKS BY C. H. SPURGEON.

My Sermon Notes. Genesis to Proverbs. 12mo., cloth.... $1.00

My Sermon Notes. Ecclesiastes to Malachi. 12mo., cloth.... $1.00

My Sermon Notes. Matthew to Acts. 12mo., cloth.... $1.00

My Sermon Notes. Romans to Revelation. 12mo., cloth $1.00

"Every paragraph opens a mine of riches."
—*Interior.*

Feathers for Arrows; or, Illustrations for Preachers and Teachers. 12mo., cloth. $1.00

The Golden Alphabet. A Devotional Commentary on the 119th Psalm. 12mo., cloth.... $1.00

Spurgeon's Gems. 12mo., cloth.... $1.00

Gleanings Among the Sheaves. 18mo., cloth, gilt top... 60

All of Grace. A book for those seeking the way of life. 16mo., paper, 30c.; cloth....... 50

According to Promise; or, The Lord's Dealings with His chosen People. 16mo., paper, 30c.; cloth 50

Twelve Christmas Sermons. 8vo., 146 pages, cloth....... 50

Twelve New Year Sermons. 8vo., 146 pages, cloth....... 50

Twelve Sermons on the Resurrection. 8vo., 146 pages, cloth..... 50

"Preachers may get aid in preparing Easter or funeral sermons from this volume. Good to present to those who have lost loved ones."—*National Baptist.*

Twelve Soul Winning Sermons. 8vo., 146 pages, cloth.... 50

Selected by Mr. Spurgeon as the twelve sermons under which there have been the most marked and permanent results.

Twelve Striking Sermons. 8vo., 146 pages, cloth....... 50

Sent Postpaid on receipt of Price.

FLEMING H. REVELL COMPANY,

CHICAGO: | NEW YORK
148 AND 150 MADISON ST. | 112 FIFTH AVE.

Publishers of Evangelical Literature.

www.ingramcontent.com/pod-product-compliance
Lightning Source LLC
Chambersburg PA
CBHW031455160426
43195CB00010BB/980